IMAGES
of America

INLAND EMPIRE AND
SAN GABRIEL VALLEY
MOVIE THEATRES

IMAGES
of America

INLAND EMPIRE AND SAN GABRIEL VALLEY MOVIE THEATRES

Kelli Shapiro, PhD

ARCADIA
PUBLISHING

Copyright © 2024 by Kelli Shapiro, PhD
ISBN 978-1-4671-0724-2

Published by Arcadia Publishing
Charleston, South Carolina

Printed in the United States of America

Library of Congress Control Number: 2021946110

For all general information, please contact Arcadia Publishing:
Telephone 843-853-2070
Fax 843-853-0044
E-mail sales@arcadiapublishing.com

Visit us on the Internet at www.arcadiapublishing.com

To those who have strived to keep historic movie theatres (and their memories) alive and in the public consciousness—whether through operation, preservation, or documentation.

CONTENTS

Acknowledgments

The author, Kelli Shapiro, began conducting the research for this book in spring 2020, when the COVID-19 pandemic started. Kelli is thankful to her Arcadia Publishing editors for providing leeway and extensions during the pandemic—when local museums, libraries, and archives were closed to the public for months or years. Kelli wants to give special thanks to the many institutions' employees and volunteers who assisted her remotely during their lengthy closures or welcomed her once they finally reopened.

Kelli owes much to the organizations and institutions that provided the book's background information, images, and ephemera. The book was especially enriched by the large and broad collections at the Theatre Historical Society of America (with thanks to its former Archives Director, Patrick Seymour); the Academy of Motion Picture Arts and Sciences' Margaret Herrick Library; the California Historical Society; the Natural History Museum's Seaver Center for Western History Research; and the Los Angeles Public Library.

Kelli applauds many organizations' efforts to digitize their archives in online databases, which made her research easier during the pandemic (and overall). Aggregators providing historical materials from multiple sources were particularly valuable—including the Media History Digital Library, Calisphere, the Online Archive of California, and the Pasadena Digital History Collaboration. Kelli also relied on newspaper databases like Newspapers.com, NewspaperArchive.com, NewsBank, and the UCR Center for Bibliographical Studies and Research's California Digital Newspapers Collection. Excellent resources included Bill Counter's "Los Angeles Theatres" blog, plus CinemaTreasures.org and CinemaTour.com (crowdsourced websites focusing on movie theater history, with accompanying Facebook groups).

Finally, Kelli wishes to thank the authors of books about the local history and/or historic theatres of Southern California, Route 66, etc.—and about the history of film exhibition and movie theatres nationally—who preceded her.

INTRODUCTION

While not nationally known for their movie theatres, like Los Angeles and Hollywood are, eastern Los Angeles County's San Gabriel Valley and the adjacent Inland Empire (encompassing Riverside and San Bernardino Counties) once boasted many architecturally impressive and culturally significant film venues. The book region, which gained national fame in the early and mid-1900s because of its position along Route 66, its mountain and desert resorts (like Big Bear and Palm Springs), and its scenic citrus groves and vineyards, was a popular destination not only for new residents and tourists but also for movie studios. Along with shooting a vast number of films in the San Gabriel Valley and Inland Empire over the years, some studios (such as Fox) owned their own theatres there. Multiple world premieres were held at local movie houses. The area also became a regular, longtime test-market for many studios' movies. At picture palaces like Riverside's Fox Theatre and San Bernardino's California Theatre, audiences frequently watched test screenings and gave crucial feedback—often while sitting beside the films' stars, directors, and studio executives. Their opinions at these sneak previews influenced what moviegoers in the rest of the country eventually saw on their own theatres' screens, affecting iconic films from *The Wizard of Oz* and *King Kong* to *Gone with the Wind*.

Beyond their unique status due to movie studios' efforts there, the Inland Empire and San Gabriel Valley are also important as a representative site. Here, film exhibition history both reflects and reveals widespread cultural, social, and demographic transformations and trends—many of which impacted not just this area but the entire country. The history of movie theatres in this region showcases national trajectories on a manageable level and is also an important subject of study itself.

Here as elsewhere in the U.S., at movie theatre evolution's beginning stages, the first places where residents could experience the magic of film were often not movie theatres—or, at least, did not start out as such. Across the area, opera houses and vaudeville venues began screening films in the early 1900s. Some retained their live-performance function while showing films intermittently or regularly, while others were transformed entirely.

Entrepreneurs also created movie showplaces where no entertainment venue previously stood— for instance, outside. Airdromes or airdomes, theatres without ceilings and sometimes without four walls, were popular in the early days of moviegoing. Most were short-lived due to issues like weather. Occasionally, the outdoor facility would be replaced by an indoor movie house onsite.

More common were indoor theatres: tiny, cheap, frequently makeshift places called nickelodeons (because of their usual five-cent pricing). Many utilized existing downtown buildings. As time passed, much new construction occurred. Older, smaller theatres often closed as nicer showplaces opened nearby—sometimes with the same owners. In 1926, when *Film Daily Year Book* offered its first state-by-state movie house list, San Gabriel Valley and Inland Empire cities offered approximately 50.

The late-1920s coming of sound caused many local theatres to shut down. Owners often could not afford the upgrades for showing "talkies." Other theatre owners not only added sound equipment but remodeled and even renamed their venues.

That coincided with the Great Depression's arrival. Its economic fallout caused numerous showplaces to shutter—some permanently, others temporarily. Still, the Great Depression led to throngs of people flocking to movie houses. Providing affordable entertainment (plus raffles, monetary contests, etc.), they offered attendees a brief escape.

The 1920s and 1930s also heralded picture palaces' rise. These large, experience-focused venues complemented elaborate designs and luxurious atmospheres with extravagant stage shows, orchestras, etc. They often offered amenities like windowed smoking rooms (where men could watch films while smoking) and cry rooms (where women could hold crying babies and not miss the movie). Generally built in larger cities with affluent populations, picture palaces' architects experimented with styles spanning the ages and the globe.

While independent movie houses were originally common, picture palaces were often owned by circuits (chains). The main local circuit was Fox West Coast, originally affiliated with the Twentieth Century Fox movie studio. Founded in 1929, it bought or opened many movie houses throughout the region (and across the state) at which to show the studio's films. Numerous local venues were called the Fox Theatre. After a Supreme Court antitrust case led to the 1948 Paramount Consent Decrees, Twentieth Century Fox divested Fox West Coast; other studios, like Paramount Pictures, also released their theatres. However, the Fox circuit's name lived on.

Another crucial local theatre owner was James Edwards, who launched his film exhibition career in 1930 in the San Gabriel Valley. Founding Edwards Theatres, he opened dozens of movie houses statewide until his 1997 death. The mogul's name still appears on about 25 multiplexes (now owned by the Regal chain).

Exhibitors' development and expansion plans were temporarily halted, and the picture palace construction era ended, during World War II. Existing movie houses played important roles in the war effort—showing newsreels, hosting war bonds drives and scrap metal or rubber collections, etc. Military bases and related facilities sprang up across the region, most including theatres where soldiers watched first-run films.

In the postwar era, car culture reigned supreme; Southern California became world-renowned for car-centric architecture. Various single-screen, freestanding movie houses opened, featuring large parking lots and Modernist architecture easy to notice from passing cars. Meanwhile, the drive-in theatre became a car culture icon, flourishing across the region (and throughout America).

Drive-ins arose on cities' outskirts and in fast-growing suburbs, especially along major thoroughfares—like Route 66's alignments, where over half a dozen drive-ins sat in the book region. Audiences began departing indoor theatres for drive-ins, which provided a casual, family-friendly environment suited to the baby boom period. Many offered children's amenities, like playgrounds. Some even held Sunday church services. Drive-ins' architects often made their exterior structures into eye-catching artworks; depictions of local history and culture frequently appeared on screen murals and marquees. By 1969, per *Film Daily Year Book*, the book region offered over thirty drive-in theatres—many of them run by the Pacific Theatres circuit.

As time passed, increasing development and rising land prices made many drive-ins unsustainable financially (both here and around the U.S.). Daytime swap meets helped, but usually not enough. While a few open drive-ins still hold swap meets, other drive-ins' flea markets outlasted the movies. Most of the area's drive-ins were destroyed—their lots more valuable for other purposes, like shopping centers. Recently, drive-in demolition has been for warehousing—a common fate for large lots in the Inland Empire, which has become one of America's primary logistics hubs.

Long before the logistics trend occurred (impacting the area's economy, employment, and land use), the Inland Empire and San Gabriel Valley had undergone other massive changes. Suburbanization was key, with new suburban developments supplanting historic downtowns as places where locals met their needs. Early malls and strip shopping centers often included movie venues. Numerous movie houses across the region and the country closed due to downtowns' abandonment, often sitting vacant for years. When governments tried to revitalize downtowns, some historic theatres got demolished during redevelopment efforts.

Suburban shopping centers, which often replaced drive-ins, provided certain features that single-screen theatres did not—but to which residents became accustomed: selection and convenience. Purpose-built multiplexes came into existence in this climate, beginning with twins and triplexes in the 1960s. (A few historic theatres locally became multiplexes earlier, creating auditoriums in backstage areas or adjacent buildings.) These frequently small, bare-bones cinemas caused the closure of innumerable historic theatres in this region and throughout the U.S.

To compete, many single-screen theatres multiplexed. Drive-ins' large lots could easily hold additional screens. Some indoor venues split their auditoriums in two, while others added screens in their balconies. Others, especially freestanding movie houses, expanded their buildings to add auditoriums. Most of the historic movie venues open today have become multi-screen operations.

Facing competition from multiplexes (along with the VCR, cable TV, etc.), many theatre operators fought to survive by turning from general audiences to niche markets. Some started offering second-run movies at bargain prices, while others hoped to attract film aficionados by playing classics. A few tried to draw highbrow attendees by switching to arthouse films. Various venues became controversial adult theatres, frequently as part of circuits. Most were fairly short-lived (as operators dealt with protests, arrests, lawsuits, etc.).

Meanwhile, as the region grew, many of its communities' demographics shifted in crucial ways. Notably, the western San Gabriel Valley became the nation's main site of Asian immigration in the 1980s and beyond. Some venues in its previously majority-white suburbs switched to screening Asian-language movies.

Regarding Latinos, certain Inland Empire movie houses had offered Spanish-language screenings regularly (weekly, etc.) for decades. These were especially found in agricultural areas where Mexican farmworkers were common. A few early theatres opened entirely to serve Hispanic audiences; like African Americans, they frequently faced segregation elsewhere, forced to sit separately. The later influx of Latino residents into these now suburban areas (and the oft-resultant white flight) led to many historic movie theatres changing fully to Spanish-language films.

In contrast, unlike many places across the U.S., the San Gabriel Valley and Inland Empire seemingly had no early movie houses geared toward an African American audience. Per trade journals' national lists, from the 1930s to the 1950s, the closest Black-oriented venues were in Los Angeles, San Diego, and San Pedro. Today, despite having adjusted to the local population's demographic transformations, none of the region's ethnic/racially focused cinemas still operate.

Although most of this book's historic theatres are gone, many have been adaptively reused for non-film purposes. Functions that utilize the theatres' auditoriums are common, such as churches, playhouses, and concert venues. Other movie houses have become banquet halls, stores, restaurants, and offices. Some look unrecognizable, while others were restored to their former glory through lengthy preservation efforts.

Very few historic movie theatres still provide locals with moviegoing opportunities today. In the San Gabriel Valley, only one historic indoor theatre and a single drive-in remain operational. Meanwhile, the Inland Empire can boasts four drive-ins and four historic movie houses open. Of those survivors, though, few remain single-screen. The one-screen film showplaces that have lasted have generally accomplished that feat because they are in isolated areas where locals have little alternative; because they are in vacation destinations where moviegoing is a fun, nostalgic activity for visitors; or both.

This book strives to tell the story of the San Gabriel Valley and Inland Empire's beloved movie theatres, including the rare surviving holdouts that still offer a communal moviegoing experience; those whose buildings host other uses; ones that sit vacant; and the many remaining only in memory (and in various collections' photographs, etc.). Although it cannot be comprehensive, the book features images of and historical details regarding almost 200 historic, originally single-screen movie venues. (With a few space-necessitated exceptions, the theatres are arranged by city in county-based chapters and arranged chronologically in city-based chapters.) Overall, the author hopes that the book will encourage readers to appreciate and support the area's historic movie houses—as well as the many museums, archives, and organizations that hold their communities' treasured histories, in which those theatres have played important roles.

One

RIVERSIDE COUNTY

On November 3, 1948, the 730-car Rubidoux Drive-in Theatre opened in unincorporated Rubidoux (now part of the city of Jurupa Valley). Architects Matcham and Heitschmidt designed the facility for Roy Hunt. The drive-in originally featured a petting zoo, playground, and miniature railroad. In 1983, it added two screens. The Rubidoux still shows first-run films today; it also holds daytime swap meets. (Courtesy of Getty Research Institute, Los Angeles, 2004.R.10.)

On May 23, 1928, Fox West Coast affiliate Principal Theaters opened Banning's 650-seat Banning Theatre with a world premiere, *Steamboat Bill, Jr.* Bob Hope hosted live radio broadcasts there in the 1940s. After a remodeling and renaming, the Fox Theatre reopened in 1953 with a sneak preview. Following its 1974-1983 closure, the Fox was multiplexed. Its balcony and stage removed, the auditorium got split in two, creating the Fox Twin Cinema. Later, a back room became a third screening area. The Fox, with its neon signage and mix of Spanish Colonial Revival and Art Deco architecture, received 1996 and 2009 renovations (partly with city redevelopment funds). Called Fox Cineplex, it plays first-run movies nightly. (Left, courtesy of Banning Library District; below, courtesy of Ken Kramer Collection, Margaret Herrick Library, Academy of Motion Picture Arts and Sciences.)

The 300-seat Banning Opera House sat beside Banning's (still standing) Coplin House hotel on San Gorgonio Avenue at Ramsey Street. Opening in March 1913, the venue's first movie screened on April 5. Per early newspaper advertisements, it offered reserved seats, with "motion pictures [and] illustrated songs" three days a week. It showed films into 1928—when the Banning Theatre arrived. Its Holcomb Building burned down. (Courtesy of Banning Library District.)

C.L. "Jimmy" James and his wife, Ida Mae, opened the Beaumont Theatre in 1940. The 400-seat movie house's blade sign is visible on the right in this postcard showing 6th Street in downtown Beaumont. It featured air conditioning and soundproofing. After its 1952 closure, the auditorium floor was flattened for the building's conversion into a rollerskating rink. Much altered, it has held the Beaumont Antique Center since the 1980s. (Courtesy of the author.)

Beaumont's 500-car Cherry Pass Drive-in Theatre opened in 1950 with a preview screening. Designed by J. Arthur Drielsma, it offered a playground, dance floor, and carhop service. Jimmy James operated it from 1952 (after closing his Beaumont Theatre) until 1955. The drive-in closed around 1969; its 1571 East 6th Street property is now a swap meet. (Courtesy of UCSB Library Geospatial Collection, Flight AXM_1967, Frame 1HH-217, May 9, 1967.)

In this photograph of early Blythe, "Airdome" is visible on the middle structure. Along with films, this airdrome (open-air movie house) also hosted sporting events, including wrestling. Its admission was 20¢–25¢. Per a 1987 *Palo Verde Valley Times* article, this image is circa 1915. 1915 is the only year that Blythe's Airdome appeared in the *Riverside City and County Directory*. (Courtesy of Palo Verde Historical Museum.)

In a page 14 photograph, the Liberty Theatre's original building sits beside Blythe's Airdome around 1915. L.B. Todd's later building (shown here) covered both Main Street properties. After buying it in 1934, Bob Dunagan often exchanged movie tickets for produce from farmers, who parked their wagons in a horse corral Dunagan established behind the 600-seat theatre. In 1946, the city condemned the operational movie house. (Courtesy of Palo Verde Historical Museum.)

The 1948 opening weekend of the second location of Bob Dunagan's Hub Theatre boasted a world premiere, *California Firebrand*. (Its star, Monte Hale, attended—along with Janet Leigh, etc.) Renamed Blythe Community Cinema, it made national news in 1989 after ejecting and banning the local newspaper's film critic over her negative reviews. Closing in the early 1990s, the 600-seat movie house, deemed unsafe, was destroyed in 2005. (Courtesy of American Classic Images.)

Bob Dunagan opened Blythe's 500-car Rancho Verde Drive-in Theatre in 1953. A decade later, the Robert L. Lippert circuit bought it and Dunagan's two other Blythe movie houses (the Hub Theatre and the still-standing, vacant, 1937 Rio Theatre at 138 South Main Street). The drive-in closed by 1991. Farmland covers its property along West Hobsonway at Defrain Boulevard. (Courtesy of UCSB Library Geospatial Collection, Flight AXM-1959, Frame 9W-14, January 1, 1959.)

This program lauded the 1950 opening of the 480-car Sunair Drive-in Theatre, adjacent to Cathedral City's Sunair housing development. It offered a western-themed screen mural, a playground, and baby-bottle warming, plus free kids' pony rides on weekends. In the 1980s, the Sunair played Spanish-language movies at least weekly and held a regular swap meet. The drive-in closed in 1987; an auto mall replaced it. (Courtesy of Palm Springs Public Library.)

J.J. Cruz opened the 550-seat, $12,000 Teatro Chapultepec beside his store on Corona's Main Street in 1926—presenting silent films, mariachi bands, Mexican plays, etc. It provided an alternative to segregated seating at Corona's California Theatre (where Latino moviegoers were relegated to the balcony) and, later, at the Corona Theatre. Local Hispanic organizations rented it for events. Ben Aranda, who operated two Spanish-language showplaces in Brawley, took over in 1935. Remodeling and renaming it the Radio Theatre, he continued its policy of showing both Spanish-language and American films. Renamed the Circle Theatre in 1936, Ben's wife Mildred managed it after his death. Closing in 1955, this center of the Latino community fell in 1970. (Both, courtesy of the Board of Trustees of the Corona Public Library.)

The segregated Corona Theatre opened in August 1929; director D.W. Griffith hosted a world premiere attended by stars like Al Jolson, Clara Bow, and Delores Del Rio. Architect Carl Boller planned Glen Harper's 1,000-seat, "atmospheric" style, Spanish Colonial Revival picture palace. After playing Spanish-language films, it closed in 1982. Preservationists prevailed against 1991 demolition plans. A church reuses it. (Courtesy of the Board of Trustees of the Corona Public Library.)

Corona's Showcase Theatre was an independent, single-screen cinema in a strip mall. It showed films from 1973 until around 1981, later gaining notoriety as an all-ages concert club. From 1993 to 2008, the Showcase played an important role in Southern California's punk scene—hosting bands like NOFX, Guttermouth, and AFI. In 2023, its strip center was undergoing redevelopment—part of a revitalization project at the adjacent Corona Mall. (Courtesy of the author.)

The Rustic Theatre has been attracting moviegoers in the artsy, mountaintop resort community of Idyllwild since 1945. The top photograph shows the venue in its first building (built in 1923). Initially owned by Bill and Prudie Underhill and later by Glenn and Nina Mae Froelich, the first Rustic had 120 seats. In 1952, the Froelichs moved the Rustic to its current location. Its former structure became an inn—now called Silver Pines Lodge. (Both buildings still resemble their original appearances.) CinemaScope equipment and a widescreen arrived in 1955. Now holding 232 seats, a stage, and a snack bar with an outdoor walk-up window, the Rustic Theatre hosts events and plays first-run movies. (Above, courtesy of Ann Congdon; below, courtesy of American Classic Images.)

The Hemet Theatre was William Martin's 1915 renaming of Hemet's 1913 Lone Star Theatre. Following 1918 earthquake damage, Martin moved it across Florida Street in 1921—opening the $30,000, Mission Revival, 400-seat movie house above. (During construction, his Airdrome played films on a nearby lot.) The showplace held a preview screening, *Follow the Leader*, in 1930. It got an Art Deco remodel in 1939; a cry room in 1951; and 3D and CinemaScope equipment in 1954. Its current, Modernist façade (below) is from the 1960s. With local multiplexes opening in 1994 and 1995, the Martin family closed their theatre. New owners showed classic, arthouse, and second-run films from 2004 to 2013. The Historic Hemet Theatre Foundation has hosted concerts, community events, and occasional movies since. (Above, courtesy of Hemet Museum; below, courtesy of American Classic Images.)

This photograph shows the 1950 construction of the $100,000 Hemacinto Drive-in Theatre, which J.W. Davis opened along Hemet's San Jacinto Road. It held 400 cars, a playground, and a stage. In 1955, the Martin family bought it, removing their circuit's last competitor. (They owned the movie houses in Hemet, San Jacinto, and Perris.) Harold Martin closed the Hemacinto in 1989; it was a vacant lot by 1992. (Courtesy of Hemet Museum.)

Indio's Egyptian Theatre opened in 1921 on Fargo Street. Judge Leroy Pawley, Indio's first mayor, later operated it with his wife, Grace. The Pawleys installed RCA Photophone sound equipment in 1930, then remodeled in 1934. The 450-seat Egyptian survived a 1938 flood (with its poster cases promoting *The Rains Came*). It did not last long thereafter. (Courtesy of Coachella Valley History Museum.)

In December 1937, Leroy Pawley opened Indio's Desert Theatre on Fargo Street at Bliss Avenue. An early program claimed that it presented "only the latest and best pictures obtainable." The 710-seat movie house showed Spanish-language films at various points, including in the 1950s and regularly throughout the 1980s. A 2020 fire turned the long-empty, boarded-up building to ruins. (Courtesy of Coachella Valley History Museum.)

This March 1960 photograph shows Indio's Aladdin Theatre after an arson fire caused $500,000 damage. Leroy Pawley's *Arabian Nights*-themed movie house opened in 1948 with 844 seats, a 500-car parking lot, and usherettes wearing Arabian costumes. Called MKA Cinema from 1980 to 1982, the Miles Avenue venue later played Spanish-language movies as the Cine-Mex. Closing in 1988, it burned in 1990. (Courtesy of USC Digital Library, *Los Angeles Examiner* Photographs Collection.)

— BEST OF SEASON'S GREETINGS TO YOU —

THIS TICKET ENTITLES HOLDER TO

ONE FREE ADMISSION

— TO THE —

INDIO DRIVE-IN Theatre

INDIO, CALIF.

6:00 P.M., Thursday, Dec. 23, 1954

THIS FREE TICKET COURTESY OF YOUR FRIENDLY INDIO MERCHANT

Indio's 500-car Coachella Valley Drive-in Theatre opened in 1952. Later changing to the Indio Drive-in, the venue added a second screen, becoming the Indio Twin in 1976. In the early 1980s, it was briefly called the Kay-Donna Drive-in. It was already closed when a 1990 fire occurred in one of its buildings—where homeless people often stayed. Its Date Avenue site now hosts a homeless-services organization. (Courtesy of the author.)

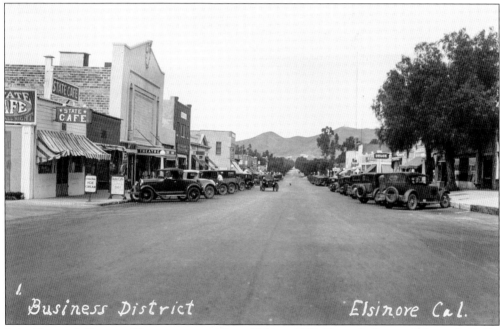

Business District   Elsinore Cal.

Lake Elsinore's Elsinore Theatre operated from 1924 to 1950. Foster Jackson and his wife, Nelle, owned it until his 1930s death; Nelle and her daughter then ran it. Per a 1945 *Boxoffice* profile, Nelle Jackson's 500-seat movie house's staff was entirely female (except the projectionist). Architect G. Stanley Wilson's Classical Revival building still stands at 117 South Main Street. (Courtesy of Ernest Marquez Collection, the Huntington Library, San Marino, California, photCL_555_06_2227.)

In 1950, Nelle Jackson, H.C. Scott, and Scott's wife opened Lake Elsinore's Lake Theatre. It offered 830 seats, air conditioning, a parking lot, a cry room, and a smoking room. A 1980 flood ended films there. The landmarked, 310 West Graham Avenue building has been the city's Lake Community Center since 1990. (Courtesy of Tom B'hend and Preston Kaufmann Collection, Margaret Herrick Library, Academy of Motion Picture Arts and Sciences.)

The United States Naval Hospital, a World War II necessity, opened at Norco's failed Lake Norconian Club resort in 1941. Its 1944 Recreation Building included a 1,200-seat theatre; injured soldiers watched first-run films, live radio broadcasts, and performances. After the hospital's 1957 closure, the state Department of Corrections operated the facility. The landmarked complex sits vacant. (Courtesy of US Navy Seabee Museum, Naval History and Heritage Command, Port Hueneme, California.)

Norco's Crest Drive-in Theatre opened in December 1968, with its Xenon system showing *The Sound of Music* on a 100-foot-tall screen. In 1983, manager Bob Cribbs stated that although the 665-car lot mostly filled up in season, only two or three carloads attended on many winter nights. Open until at least 1988, the 2400 Hamner Avenue drive-in disappeared in the 1990s. (Photograph by Gary Evans. Courtesy of Gary's Norco Pics.)

In Palm Springs' 1920s El Paseo shopping center, the El Paseo Theatre opened in 1930. Sometimes called the Little Theatre, it had under 300 seats. After a 1933 closure, new operator Earle Strebe reopened the movie house in 1935, doubling its capacity and giving it a remodeling by architect Clifford A. Balch in 1937. The theatre closed around 1960; a restaurant now reuses its space. (Courtesy of Palm Springs Historical Society.)

PLAZA
PALM SPRINGS
EL PASEO
THEATRES

• Program •

MAR. 23 - MAR. 30
INCLUSIVE

Phone 4384
(Connects All Theatres)

Palm Springs Theatre
3 SHOWS DAILY
3-7-9 P.M.
Box Office Opens
Matinee 2:45
Eves. 6:45
Cont. Sun. from 1:45

Plaza Theatre
2 SHOWS DAILY
2 P. M. — 8 P. M.

El Paseo Theatre
2 Shows Nightly
7 and 9
Doors Open 6:45

Earle Strebe operated the 600-seat Palm Springs Theatre from 1932 (when it opened with *Lawyer Man*, whose star, William Powell, was in attendance) to 1974. Renamed the Village Theatre in the 1940s, the Palm Canyon Drive movie house got twinned in 1977. It and surrounding historic buildings were razed in 1984 for the expansion of Desert Fashion Plaza, a now-destroyed indoor mall. (Courtesy of Palm Springs Historical Society.)

In this photograph, local theatre magnate Earle Strebe and his family cut a cake depicting his Palm Springs Drive-in on Ramon Road. Its 1964 grand opening featured the world premiere of Disney's *The Three Lives of Thomasina*. With horseback riding a popular desert activity, the 800-car drive-in welcomed equestrians—offering buckets of oats, watering troughs, and hitching posts for horses. It closed in 1989. (Courtesy of Palm Springs Historical Society.)

Palm Springs' 1936 Plaza Theatre is part of developer Julia Carnell's La Plaza shopping center. Architect Harry Williams designed the Spanish Colonial Revival picture palace's air-conditioned, "atmospheric" auditorium—resembling a village under a starry sky. Costars Greta Garbo and Robert Taylor attended its opening world premiere, *Camille*. Later, celebrities hosted national radio broadcasts there. 1949 brought a Cycloramic screen. Original operator Earle Strebe ran the Plaza until 1974. Metropolitan Theatres twinned the auditorium and removed the ticket booth in 1977, leading to the city's Historic Site Preservation Board's founding. Movies ended in 1989. The Fabulous Palm Springs Follies variety show played there 1991–2014. The city bought the landmarked, 800-seat theatre in 2015. By late 2023, the Palm Springs Plaza Theatre Foundation raised $15.2 million toward a 2024 restoration and 2025 reopening. (Both, courtesy of Palm Springs Historical Society.)

The Camelot Theatre opened on February 4, 1967—showing *Dr. Zhivago* at a celebrity-filled, $100-per-couple benefit. Metropolitan Theatres' $750,000 movie house, built in the Palm Springs Shopping Center's parking lot, featured Modernist architecture by Mayer and Kanner. The Camelot offered an upstairs lounge; an art gallery; a curved, 68-foot, floor-to-ceiling widescreen; and a D-150 All-Purpose Projection System meant for playing 70mm and CinemaScope. A 1971 expansion added a second auditorium—later split in two. After its 1992 closure, the triplex reopened as the Festival of Arts Theatres in 1999. Named the Camelot again in 2002, the Palm Springs Cultural Center's venue is renowned for its arthouse and repertory screenings (some in 70mm), film festivals, and special events. However, in 2022 (due to the COVID-19 pandemic's effects), the nonprofit stopped playing first-run films there. (Both, courtesy of Palm Springs Historical Society.)

An open-air movie venue operated in 1930s Perris. In 1946, the $75,000 Perris Theatre replaced that airdrome at 295 South D Street. By the early 1990s, it showed Spanish-language films. After years of church usage, the city bought the 400-seat movie house. Despite a 2010 exterior renovation of architect S. Charles Lee's Art Deco building, the Perris Theatre sits vacant because of infrastructure issues. (Courtesy of Library of Congress, LC-MA05-445 [P&P].)

The *San Jacinto Register* announced in October 1912 that Harry Courtright was turning a former bowling alley/billiard hall into the Temple Theatre. It noted that the Main Street movie house would have a separate entrance for "Mexicans and Indians, who will be seated by themselves." In 1914, new proprietor W.B. Walker bought a new projector. An IOOF group used the Temple as its lodge in 1915. (Courtesy of the author.)

Main Street, Looking East, San Jacinto, Cal.

San Jacinto's Soboba Theatre was one of the region's most architecturally unique venues. Named after the nearby Soboba Indian Reservation and the Soboba people, its Native American theme encompassed Frederic Johnson's Pueblo Revival architecture; homemade interior décor; and ushers' uniforms. Oscar "Harry" Hofman and Lester Reynolds opened the $75,000 venue in 1927. Its opening boasted California's first screening of Cecil B. DeMille's *The Country Doctor*, plus vaudeville. Sid Grauman, of Hollywood's similarly thematic Grauman's Chinese Theatre, attended. The Soboba featured over 700 seats, a Kilgen Wonder Organ, a cry room, and earphones for hard-of-hearing attendees. William Martin bought the Soboba in 1941. Renamed the San Jacinto Theatre, the movie house closed in 1954. It burned down in 1968. (Above, courtesy of the author; below, courtesy of Special Collections & University Archives, University of California, Riverside.)

Two

CITY OF RIVERSIDE

The Rubidoux Theatre was one of Roy Hunt's many Riverside movie houses; his wife, Blodwen, ran its box office. Operating as the Grand in 1913, it gained the new name in 1923. It sponsored an employee baseball team called the Rubidoux Rubes. The 420-seat Rubidoux became California's third movie venue with sound in 1927. Closing in 1938, its 3827 Main Street building is gone. (Courtesy of Museum of Riverside, Riverside, California.)

Charles Loring opened one of Southern California's earliest opera houses, Riverside's Loring Opera House, in 1890. It hosted performers like Sarah Bernhardt, John Philip Sousa, and W.C. Fields. In 1915, it held test screenings of D.W. Griffith's *The Clansman* (soon retitled *Birth of a Nation*). After a $25,000 remodeling by architect G. Stanley Wilson, it became the 1,100-seat Loring Theatre in 1918. Operator Roy Hunt renamed it the Golden State Theatre in 1928, reopening it with Al Jolson's talkie, *The Singing Fool*. Before its 1973 closure, the Golden State was playing sexploitation flicks for an adults-only audience. The theatre's portion of the Loring Building was razed after a 1990 fire; the rest of the landmarked structure survives along Mission Inn Avenue at Main Street. (Both, courtesy of Ken Kramer Collection, Margaret Herrick Library, Academy of Motion Picture Arts and Sciences.)

At 1075 Main Street, across from the Riverside Historic Courthouse, once sat the Auditorium Theatre. It hosted vaudeville and regularly screened films by 1909, when it was called O'Dette's Picture Auditorium (for manager Rae O'Dette). In 1912, it remodeled. In 1916, renamed the Orpheum Theatre, the movie house previewed D.W. Griffith's *Intolerance*. It got a new name, the Mission Theatre, in 1923. It closed around 1928. (Courtesy of Riverside Public Library.)

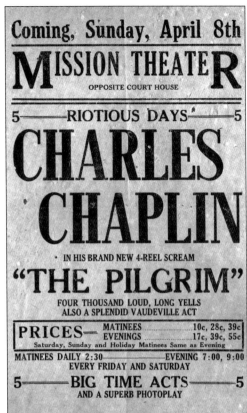

The Star Theatre's painted sign is visible on the right. Located in a former planing mill building at 575 Eighth Street, that movie house was operating by 1908 as the Palace of Pictures. The 1909 city directory revealed a brief name change to the Crystal Theatre. On February 27, 1909, it reopened— remodeled—as the Star. Until around 1912, the Star hosted films, illustrated songs, and performers. (Courtesy of the author.)

Beside G. Rouse's department store, "Theatre" signage once hung above the Regent Theatre's arched entry on Main Street, just south of Eighth Street. Planned by J.W. Carroll for George Frost in 1914, the $75,000 movie house offered 800 seats, including boxes. In 1924, Roy Hunt bought the Regent; by 1925, its façade had a marquee. A Kress five-and-dime store replaced the Regent by 1930. (Courtesy of Riverside Public Library.)

The West Coast Theatres circuit's 1,550-seat West Coast Riverside Theatre opened in 1929. It boasted sound films, a 19-person orchestra with a Wurlitzer organ, and Mission Revival and Spanish Colonial Revival architecture—designed by Balch and Stanbery, collaborating with L.A. Smith. Fox West Coast soon renamed the picture palace the Fox Riverside. (Courtesy of Bison Archives.)

The Fox Riverside Theatre was renowned for its test screenings. Its tower's neon "Preview" signage (visible here) lit up to alert locals that one would occur. Most notable was *Gone with the Wind*, which test-screened in 1939 with producer David O. Selznick attending. *Ocean's 11* and *The Lost Weekend* also previewed there. The Fox hosted vaudeville and community events as well. During World War II, amidst local military bases' housing shortage, manager Roy Hunt let servicemen sleep in the Fox's lobby and aisles. New lessees played Spanish-language and Spanish-subtitled films from 1978 to 1994. In the 1990s, the (otherwise vacant) Fox hosted various arthouse movie series and film festivals. The city seized the empty, landmarked building via eminent domain in 2004. After a $35 million restoration, it reopened in 2010 as the Fox Performing Arts Center. (Courtesy of Library of Congress, LC-MA05-5774 [P&P].)

In 1942, Fox West Coast's Lido Theatre opened in what was previously the Fox Riverside Theatre's stagehouse and offices (at the Fox's west end). Despite sharing a building, the Lido was considered a separate venue. It had its own marquee, box office, snack bar, restrooms, etc. Architect Clifford A. Balch designed the $50,000 facility, which had 540 seats, including 140 in a balcony. The Lido played second-run movies for years, as its original operator, Roy Hunt, intended. Renamed Stage One, it screened arthouse films from 1966 until 1972. It reopened in 1978 as a Pussycat Theatre, part of the statewide Pussycat circuit of adults-only movie houses. In 1991, it switched from X-rated to second-run movies. Retitled the Metro Theatre, the venture was short-lived. This secondary film space later became the renovated, reopened picture palace's backstage area again. (Courtesy of American Classic Images.)

Architect S. Charles Lee designed Riverside's $150,000, Streamline Moderne style De Anza Theatre. Opening in 1939 with *Young Mr. Lincoln*, Roy Hunt's 1,000-seat movie house featured wooden bas reliefs (below) representing its namesake, Spanish explorer Juan Bautista de Anza. After first-run screenings ended there in 1981, the De Anza played Spanish-language and second-run films, then became a concert club—hosting nationally touring rock bands. A market has occupied the 4225 Market Street building since 1988. The landmarked structure's exterior looks much as it did in the theatre's heyday. (Above, courtesy of the author; below, courtesy of Getty Research Institute, Los Angeles, 2004.R.10 [Job Lee-DE].)

March Field (later March Air Force Base) added multiple buildings in an expansion beginning in 1928. Additions included the $25,000 War Department Theatre, which featured Mission Revival style architecture, air conditioning, and sound equipment for "talkies." One of many movie houses the U.S. Army Motion Picture Service operated on bases, it screened films every day except Sunday by 1934. It later served as March's Cultural Center. (Courtesy of the author.)

Riverside's Camp Anza, the U.S. Army's World War II staging camp for soon-to-deploy soldiers, operated from 1942 to 1946. Lieutenant Kenneth Buckridge managed its Theater One, a wooden-bench venue that played not only first-run films but pre-releases (and held performances). In this aerial photograph, Theater One is the large building above the sport courts, to the right of the arched-roof gymnasium. It no longer stands. (Courtesy of Riverside Public Library.)

The Chatterbox Theatre opened on June 27, 1941, at 3812 Van Buren Boulevard in the Arlington neighborhood. Per locals, its name and sign came from the closed Chatterbox restaurant. Owner Bob Elder, who did projection at Camp Anza's Theater One, would sometimes take its films to screen at the 398-seat Chatterbox. The small, independent movie house survived until at least 1952. (Courtesy of Museum of Riverside, Riverside, California.)

The 705-seat Arlington Theatre opened on Magnolia Avenue near Van Buren Boulevard in 1946. The neighborhood movie house featured Modernist architecture, air conditioning, and a balcony–plus that key postwar amenity, a parking lot. After closing in 1987, it became a concert club, then a store. The city demolished the boarded-up building around 1995, but its plans to build a new library there fell through. (Courtesy of American Classic Images.)

The Magnolia Drive-in Theatre was located in Riverside's Arlington neighborhood, along Magnolia Avenue west of Tyler Street. Architect J. Arthur Drielsma designed the 475-car theatre. According to *Variety*, its 1950 grand opening featured appearances by unnamed "pic celebs." Closed in 1984, a police station and ice-skating rink replaced it. (Courtesy of UCSB Library Geospatial Collection, Flight RCFC, Frame 87, June 24, 1963.)

Riverside's Van Buren Drive-in Theatre sits on a former orange grove site on Van Buren Boulevard. Its 1964 opening offered a double feature, *The Patsy* and *The Carpetbaggers*. Two more screens came in 1975. Remodeling occurred in 2006-2007; digital projection arrived in 2015. Today, the Van Buren offers first-run films, plus a swap meet. (Courtesy of Riverside Public Library.)

Special Evening Till Dawn Show

EVERY FRIDAY NITE — ALL SUMMER

Giant Triple Feature Program

ADMIT 1 CARLOAD FREE

Pass Good At Either of These Theatres

MISSION DRIVE-IN
POMONA

VAN BUREN DRIVE-IN
RIVERSIDE

From About 10:30 Till Dawn

DATE _8/27_

Three

SAN BERNADINO COUNTY

In 1950, the Western Amusement circuit's $100,000 Barstow Theatre opened at 140 West Main Street (Route 66) in Barstow. Its features included architecture by Howard George Elwell, a Cycloramic screen, two cry rooms, and 750 seats. The movie house's auditorium got multiplexed in 1976. Called Barstow Twin Cinemas or Barstow Cinema I and II, it closed in 1988 and was demolished in 1996. (Courtesy of American Classic Images.)

Barstow's Fletcher Opera House opened in 1909. Owner/operator Mary Fletcher's 300-seat venue played films by 1914. The Fletcher may have also been called the Amuse Theatre, which appeared in a directory that year at the address this postcard listed (Elm Street's block number 1). Sold in 1920 and renamed the Liberty, the venue burned down on Christmas in 1922. (Courtesy of San Bernardino County Museum.)

This postcard shows the Forum Theatre's second Barstow location at 203 East Main Street, where it moved in 1936. The building held 405 seats, up from 180. In 1947, three movie studios sued Forum operator W.E. Cox over unpaid bills; the federal lawsuit got dismissed in 1948, after he paid. The Forum closed in 1960. (Courtesy of Seaver Center for Western History Research, Los Angeles County Museum of Natural History.)

'Camp Irwin's huge outdoor theatre. Here the latest in motion pictures are shown nightly with an occasional special show presented by famed Hollywood celebrities.

This vintage postcard depicts the packed movie theatre/performance venue at Camp Irwin, an army base near Barstow. Theatres have long been a popular amenity at American military bases—whether indoors or, like Camp Irwin's, outdoors. Opening in 1940 as the Mojave Anti-Aircraft Range, the desert facility received its Camp Irwin name in 1942. It is now the Fort Irwin National Training Center. (Courtesy of Riverside Public Library.)

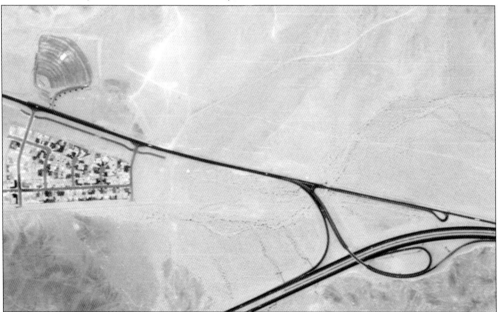

Barstow's Skyline Drive-in Theatre has shown films along Route 66 since 1966. Its September 30th grand opening offered a double feature, free candy for kids, and free Cokes for everyone. Originally operated by Western Amusement, it sat closed from 1988 until 1996. New owner Larry Rodkey added a second screen in 2000 and digital projectors in 2015. (Courtesy of UCSB Library Geospatial Collection, Flight TG-3358, Frame 30, July 17, 1973.)

Frank Johnson's $20,000 Grizzly Theatre opened along Village Drive in Big Bear Lake (then called Pine Knot) in 1920. Initially, the 500-seat movie house's two Simplex projectors exclusively played First National films. Leaning into its mountain resort locale, the Grizzly received attention in film exhibition journals for its unique, tree-centric theme inside and out—with the auditorium resembling an arbor. The rustic, wooden building burned down in 1941. (Courtesy of the author.)

Big Bear City's 1930 Peter Pan Woodland Club, a $250,000 private club/resort, offered its members many amenities. One was the 312-seat Peter Pan Theatre, which played movies nightly (in season) upstairs in the clubhouse. The movie venue's 1946 newspaper advertisement touted it as "the place to be," providing "a good show for the entire family." The clubhouse burned down in 1948. (Courtesy of the author.)

You Are Invited to Visit

Peter Pan Club

BIG BEAR CITY

∗∗∗∗∗∗∗∗∗∗∗∗

Outstanding Food and Cocktails

∗∗∗∗∗∗∗∗∗∗∗∗

Swimming, Motion Pictures,
Golfing, Tennis, Ping Pong

∗∗∗∗∗∗∗∗∗∗∗∗

Moonlight Rides and Barbecues

∗∗∗∗∗∗∗∗∗∗∗∗

Open Until October 15
Closed Every Monday

The recreation building at Stillwell's, a popular Big Bear lakefront resort, held a 200-seat movie venue. Called the Log Cabin Theatre or the Stillwell Country Club Theatre, it was open before June 1930, when it played its first talkie. Equipment problems soon caused silent pictures to return. Stillwell's was still regularly screening films when this brochure was made during World War II. Its building burned in 1945. (Courtesy of the author.)

HOMELIKE ATMOSPHERE

ON THE BEACH AT STILLWELL'S

NO CALIFORNIA excursion is complete without at least one stay at Stillwell's-on-the-Lake-Front. This is the universal testimony of tourists. With sport as a first consideration for the vacation, no item has been overlooked. Fishing and hunting in season, of course; camp fire parties, canoeing, hiking, motor-boating, swimming and motor tours entice, and dancing to good music affords unalloyed pleasure to all, whether you dance or not. A tennis court of concrete awaits you, if so disposed. Afternoon Bridge Tea parties in lounging room. The hostess, Mrs. Mamie Stillwell, arranges bridge tournaments, tennis tournaments, horse-back riding parties and hiking parties. For 23 years she has successfully promoted a feeling of goodfellowship among the guests. Silver cup trophies are awarded tournament winners. Stillwell's also operates the only all-talkie theatre at Big Bear Lake. Here you will find Anna Stillwell, who is always ready to serve you and to see that the latest pictures are shown.

We have a small grocery store at camp. We are only a few blocks from large markets and metropolitan prices.

SADDLE HORSES

Saddle horses are available nearby at 75c to $1.00 per hour.

BETWEEN SEASON VACATIONS

Don't forget to spend a vacation at Stillwell's—in the Fall or in the Spring. These are the in-between seasons, and our rates are considerably lower on both modern cottages and the unmodern cabins.

After a day of deer or duck hunting, or a day of rabbit hunting in the desert, it is a real pleasure to return to our cozy lounge, with its open fireplace, for rest and relaxation. You'll always find a jolly, congenial crowd in the lounge room, enjoying a weiner bake, popcorn popping or a marshmallow roast.

For Additional Information Address

STILLWELL'S

CARL W. and MAMIE STILLWELL, Owners and Managers
Big Bear Lake, California   Phone: No. 2421 Big Bear

SUNSET FROM STILLWELL'S VERANDA   "Frazier" Photo

Earle Strebe's Big Bear Theatre opened in April 1946. S. Charles Lee designed its steel and reinforced concrete building. Along with films (including a late-night horror show on Saturdays), it hosted community events. By 1959, the 700-seat venue provided CinemaScope movies. Strebe owned it into the 1970s. The Big Bear Theatre was still operating in 1988; fire later destroyed it. (Courtesy of the author.)

Calico Ghost Town once offered visitors a movie venue. In the 1950s, Walter Knott (of Knotts Berry Farm fame) turned Calico—an abandoned silver mining community near Barstow—into a tourist attraction. In 1967, an existing building was remodeled into the Nickelodeon, which played early silent films for visitors. Also called the Silver Nugget Theatre, it was still operating in 1975. It was later renamed the Calikage Playhouse. (Courtesy of the author.)

In 1910, Fred Dawes opened Chino's Dawes Theatre. Per 1910 advertisements, it offered "moving pictures, illustrated songs and music" nightly for 10¢. For five more cents, patrons could get "reserved seats on a raised platform." In 1911, L.D. Jones and Joe Brinderson bought and renamed the Dawes as the Chino Theatre. Its brick building stands at 5216 D Street. (Courtesy of Chino's Old Schoolhouse Museum.)

L.D. Jones and Joe Brinderson opened Chino's 375-seat, vaudeville-oriented Vaudette Theatre (above) in 1912. By 1919, directories listed it as the Chino Theatre. (The prior Chino Theatre presumably already closed.) In 1926, new owner Ashley L. Woods renamed it the Woods Theatre. His 1937 expansion and remodeling brought 500 seats, a smoking room, and a cry room, plus Art Deco architecture (right). The venue played Spanish-language films regularly (but not exclusively) from 1934 until the 1960s. Renamed the Center Theatre in 1949, its reopening advertisement touted "movie stars in person, plus 2 big first run pictures and vodvil" [vaudeville]. Later called the Woods again, movies ended by 1967, when the auditorium became the Woods Playhouse. Later holding retail, its 6th Street building is gone. (Both, courtesy of Chino's Old Schoolhouse Museum.)

Chino's third venue to be called the Chino Theatre, owned by Jack and Arnold Anderson, opened in 1947. The "gala premiere" and "Paramount studio preview" promoted on its opening night marquee (above) was for a Bob Hope comedy, *Where There's Life*. S. Charles Lee designed the $200,000, California redwood building with Art Deco and Late Moderne elements. From 1958 to 1959, a Girl Scout troop (and the girls' parents) operated the 780-seat movie house as a fundraiser. The Chino Bowl bowling alley reused the space from 1960 until 1988. The 12931 Central Avenue building (now vacant) held retail from 1992 to 2022. In 2009, the city used $15,000 in redevelopment funds to restore and relight the former theatre's red, neon "Chino" signage. (Both, courtesy of S. Charles Lee Papers, UCLA Library Special Collections, Charles E. Young Research Library, University of California, Los Angeles.)

This photograph of Colton's Eighth Street (now La Cadena Drive) shows the Hub City Theatre. Opening in 1913 as the Crescent, it became the Argonne in 1919, then the Colton Theatre in 1922—reopening as the Hub City after the New Colton Theatre's 1939 opening nearby. The 600-seat movie house played Spanish-language films often from around 1943 until its 1955 closure. Destruction came in 1959. (Courtesy of San Bernardino County Museum.)

Crestline's Crestline Village Theatre opened in 1937. Earl Strebe owned the 350-seat, Quonset hut-style movie house for decades. In 1998, it sneak-previewed Disney's *The Parent Trap* remake, which had filmed many scenes in the area. Movies ended by 2003. After hosting plays and church services, the building sat vacant by 2012. In 2022, a production company moved in. (Courtesy of Frashers Fotos Collection/HJG and Pomona Public Library, Pomona, California.)

Glen Harper's 1937, $45,000 Fontana Theatre offered 750 seats, air conditioning, and a cry room. Carl Boller's Art Deco architecture and freestanding marquee survive. Beginning in the 1950s, the building held commercial uses, becoming a playhouse from 1999 to 2022. Rocker Sammy Hagar started remodeling it into a concert club in 2023. (Courtesy of Tom B'hend and Preston Kaufmann Collection, Margaret Herrick Library, Academy of Motion Picture Arts and Sciences.)

S. Charles Lee designed Glen Harper's second Fontana movie house, the 1948 Harper Theatre, with a Lamella barrel roof and 50-foot tower. 1949 advertisements for the 700-seat, $100,000, second-run venue encouraged locals, "Wait and see two big hits for less money." The 8470 Nuevo Street building has hosted churches for decades. (Courtesy of S. Charles Lee Papers, UCLA Library Special Collections, Charles E. Young Research Library, University of California, Los Angeles.)

This matchbook lists the Pussycat Theatres circuit's adult movie houses. The Fontana Pussycat began as the 1949 Arrow Theatre, which Howard E. Jones designed for Robert Jones. The 800-seat, $120,000 Arrow became the Pussycat in August 1970, showing X-rated films until 1974. As the Fontana Family Theatre and the Del Mar Family Theatre, it played second-run movies and Spanish-language films during the 1980s. Churches have since utilized the building. (Courtesy of the author.)

PARIS PUSSYCAT THEATRE
930 National Ave. - National City

PUSSYCAT THEATRE
740 - 4th Ave. - San Diego

PUSSYCAT WORLD THEATRE
914 Ninth Street - Sacramento

ART-CINEMA
1118-20 Broadway - Oakland

THE MOVIE THEATRE
345 Ocean Blvd. - Long Beach

LYRIC THEATRE
7208 Pacific Blvd. - Huntington Park

PARK THEATRE
21622 Sherman Way - Canoga Park

GARDEN THEATRE
304 E. Lincoln - Anaheim

PUSSYCAT THEATRE
1653 Cravens - Torrance

PUSSY CAT THEATRE
444 So. Hill - Los Angeles

SUNSET THEATRE
1508 No. Western - Hollywood

PUSSYCAT THEATRE
1442 2nd St. - Santa Monica

PUSSYCAT THEATRE
7734 Santa Monica. Bl.-Hollywood

PUSSYCAT THEATRE
167779 Arrow Blvd. - Fontana

CONTINENTAL THEATRE
Phoenix, Arizona

PUSSYCAT THEATRE   1970

(U) 126

Fontana's now-gone Bel-Air Drive-in opened at 15895 Valley Boulevard in 1956—screening *Love Me Tender*, Elvis's debut, on a Cycloramic screen. In 1957, multiple churches held an Easter service there. The approximately 1,000-car Bel-Air played X-rated movies in 1968, if not longer. Its operator since 1962, Pacific Theatres, showed family-friendly films there before its 1989 closure. (Courtesy of UCSB Library Geospatial Collection, Flight AXM_1959, Frame 15w-51, 1959.)

Sitting on Highland's Baseline Street, the Baseline Drive-in Theatre offered 700 car spaces and 300 seats. Its October 1948 grand opening presented Lucille Ball in *Her Husband's Affairs* and Johnny Weissmuller in *Tarzan and the Huntress*. The Pacific Theatres venue closed in 1989, then burned down. (© Elisa Leonelli. Courtesy of Elisa Leonelli Collection, H.Mss.1102. Special Collections, The Claremont Colleges Library, Claremont, California.)

Lake Arrowhead's 350-seat Village Theatre (sometimes called the Arrowhead Theatre) opened in 1938 inside an expansion of the popular, 1922 Lake Arrowhead Village development. Early advertisements stated the showplace was "dedicated to lovers of the Silver Screen." It was part of Earle Strebe's local circuit until at least 1974. The tourist-focused shopping/entertainment complex, with its Norman English architecture, was intentionally burned in a 1979 fire department training exercise. (Courtesy of the author.)

On Lake Arrowhead's shore, behind the Village Boathouse, sat the Ye Jester Theatre—a 400-seat airdrome (open-air movie venue). Operated by Anthony Burke and then Dr. Ralph L. Power, it combined rustic elements with a Norman English, outdoor playhouse atmosphere. During summers, it showed films nightly from 1925 until at least 1928. (Courtesy of Spence Air Photos, the Benjamin and Gladys Thomas Air Photo Archives, University of California, Los Angeles.)

The Bar-Len Drive-in Theatre was located on Lenwood Road (Route 66) in Lenwood, outside Barstow—with its moniker a combination of both. The $90,000 venue opened on December 29, 1948. The Western Amusement circuit operated the 400-car, single-screen, second-run theatre until its early 1980s closure. The Bar-Len was later destroyed. (Courtesy of the author.)

Loma Linda's Drive-in Theatre opened August 20, 1939—shutting down in 1940 after the world's first drive-in (New Jersey's 1933 Park-in Theatres) sued owners M.A. Rogers and Thomas Burgess, claiming patent infringement. Reopening in 1947 as the 99 Drive-in, it became the Tri-City in 1948. Known for its screen mural, Pacific Theatres' venue showed Spanish-language movies weekly by 1975. It closed in 1993. (Courtesy of Library of Congress, LC-MA05-6103 [P&P].)

For its May 1956 opening, Montclair's $300,000 Mission Drive-in Theatre showed *Picnic* on its Cinemascope screen. The 1,350-car facility at Mission Boulevard and Ramona Avenue added three screens in 1975, getting renamed the Mission Tiki in 2006. Developers purchased it in 2019 for warehouse usage, but the COVID-19 pandemic stalled redevelopment. The drive-in closed and fell in 2023. (Courtesy of UCSB Library Geospatial Collection, Flight C-23870, Frame 2496, 1960.)

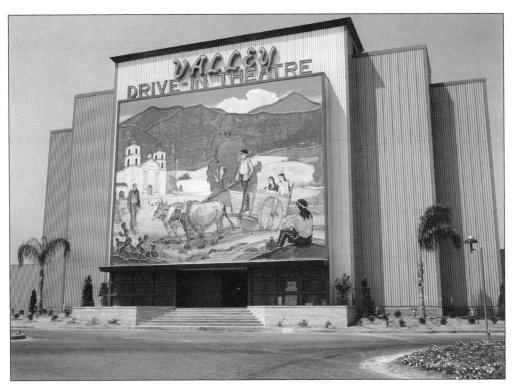

The Valley Drive-in opened in 1948 on Holt Boulevard at Central Avenue in then-unincorporated Montclair. Its screen tower featured what was reportedly the world's largest neon mural: 2,500 feet of neon depicting an early California mission scene. The 650-car theatre also boasted caged monkeys and a playground. In 1977, the Valley closed and was bulldozed, replaced by a car dealership. (Courtesy of Ontario City Library.)

C.A. Simons's 1930 Needles Theatre sits at 823 West Broadway Street (Route 66), inside Needles's Masonic Temple (a Spanish Colonial Revival and Moorish building by DeWitt Mitcham). The 700-seat showplace offered a pipe organ, cooling system, and stage. Cartoonist Charles Schulz, creator of *Peanuts*, watched films there while growing up nearby. Closing around 1985, the long-vacant theatre's neon marquee got restored and relit in 2008. (Courtesy of Needles Regional Museum.)

The Liberty Theatre was operating by 1918 on Main Street in Needles. As of 1921, proprietor C.A. Simons also ran movie houses in two other Route 66 towns: Barstow's Liberty Theatre and Oatman, Arizona's Oatman Theatre. In 1928, Simons's Needles Liberty hosted events like a dance contest and a raffle for a coin-filled chest. The 600-seat venue closed in the early 1930s. (Courtesy of Needles Regional Museum.)

Harry Milling opened Ontario's 300-seat Euclid Photoplay in 1911 at 137 North Euclid Avenue. In 1915, he took over and renamed Jacob Lerch's 1913 Isis Theatre in this still-standing, landmarked, 120 North Euclid building. The new, over 500-seat Euclid Photoplay showed films on Sundays in 1919–1920, challenging Ontario's Sabbath-closure ordinance (known as "blue laws"). Later called the Forum and the Park, it closed around 1962. (Courtesy of Ontario City Library.)

G. Stanley Wilson designed Ontario's $30,000 California Theatre for Dr. C. McClelland in 1919. The independent, 974-seat, 136 North Euclid Avenue venue received a 1940 remodel. Renamed the Ritz Theatre in 1961, it played B-movies and second-run fare. Around 1968, X-rated films arrived. A 1970 police raid occurred simultaneously at it and another adult, single-screen cinema in the book region, San Bernardino's 1968 Fine Arts Theatre. By 1971, the Ritz and Fine Arts were part of the Alley Cat circuit, bought by porn film producer C. Tobalina Productions. Amber Theatres—a woman-owned circuit focused on attracting females and couples to adult movie houses—took over both in 1973. 1974 advertisements promoted Amber's weekly "Ladies Nite" at the retitled Ritz Fine Arts. It burned in 1979. (Both, courtesy of Ontario City Library.)

West Coast Theatres opened Ontario's Granada Theatre in 1926. Architect L.A. Smith's Spanish Colonial Revival venue was part of Dr. Calvert Emmons's $200,000 Emmons Building. After closing it in 1932 (presumably due to the Great Depression), Fox West Coast provided a 1936 Art Deco remodel—adding the current marquee (above) and a new snack bar (below). During World War II, the 974-seat Granada held a war bond drive, a rubber collection effort, etc. Spanish-language movies played there from around 1978 into the early 1980s. Following a $60,000 renovation in 1990, the auditorium hosted concerts for years. The city landmarked the 303 North Euclid Avenue structure in 1998. Churches reused it throughout the 2000s; classic films nights occurred in 2009–2010, at least. The Inland Conservatory for the Performing Arts has utilized the Granada since 2016. (Both, courtesy of Ontario City Library.)

The 1300-seat Wyatt Opera House in Redlands opened in 1904, part of H.C. Wyatt's regional circuit. The Mission Revival style performance venue started showing films in 1916, when its lessees constructed a projection booth (with Powers 6B projectors) in the balcony. Later called the Wyatt Theatre, it was demolished in 1929, having been deemed unsafe and condemned in 1928. (Courtesy of USC Digital Library, California Historical Society Collection.)

Redlands' Majestic Theatre opened at 502 Orange Street in 1911 as a performance venue. Closed briefly amidst a 1912 polio outbreak, it showed films by 1914. Inland Theatres operated it until 1925—when Fox West Coast affiliate Junior Theatres took over the Majestic, Wyatt, and Liberty. Following a 1928 condemnation, the 650-seat Majestic reopened in 1931. It shut down again before 1939. (Courtesy of the Archives, A.K. Smiley Public Library.)

In 1912, Redlands' indoor swimming facility on State Street at Fourth Street, the Natatorium, got converted into the Empress Theatre. Renamed the Liberty in 1923, it became the 490-seat State Theatre around 1939. Fox West Coast gave it new equipment (including air conditioning) and an Art Deco remodel, reopening it as the first-run Loma Theatre in 1943. Reused as a store since 1958, the theatre was among six historic business blocks demolished in a downtown redevelopment project—making way for the 1977 Redlands Mall. That indoor shopping center also died, shuttering in 2010. As of 2023, the city planned to raze it for a mixed-use development. (Above, courtesy of the Archives, A.K. Smiley Public Library; below, courtesy of Ken Kramer Collection, Margaret Herrick Library, Academy of Motion Picture Arts and Sciences.)

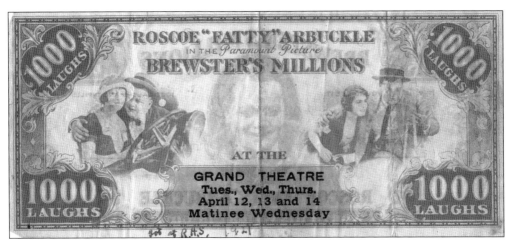

This dollar-shaped flyer promoted the Grand Theatre's showing of the 1921 comedy *Brewster's Millions*. The Grand opened in 1910 on Orange Street at Stuart Street in Redlands. It reopened in July 1920—apparently at a different location, 102 West State Street—playing *Alias Miss Dodd*. Briefly called the New Grand, it featured a new organ. It was out of business by 1926. (Courtesy of the Archives, A.K. Smiley Public Library.)

In 1941, Clifford A. Balch transformed the Fox Redlands Theatre's backstage area into another film venue, the 486-seat Grove Theatre. From 1952 to 1980, it served as the Redlands Footlighters' playhouse. Renamed the Rainbow Theatre, it showed movies again in the 1980s-1990s. The 24 East Vine Street space now holds a restaurant. (Courtesy of Tom B'hend and Preston Kaufmann Collection, Margaret Herrick Library, Academy of Motion Picture Arts and Sciences.)

West Coast Theatres' $400,000 Redlands picture palace, the Redlands Theatre, featured 1,505 seats, a Wurlitzer organ, and Spanish Colonial Revival architecture by L.A. Smith. Opened in 1928, it got sound and the Fox Redlands name in 1929. Fox West Coast turned the stage house into a separate movie showplace, the Grove Theatre, in 1941. The Fox's balcony gained two 80-inch screens in 1981. The 123 Cajon Street triplex closed in the 1980s. In 2004, an office moved into the long-vacant space. The Fox Event Center, a banquet facility and concert venue, has utilized the auditorium since 2009. (Above, courtesy of the Archives, A.K. Smiley Public Library; below, courtesy of Tom B'hend and Preston Kaufmann Collection, Margaret Herrick Library, Academy of Motion Picture Arts and Sciences.)

Rialto's 675-car Foothill Drive-in Theatre, designed by architect Howard E. Jones, opened in 1949 along Foothill Boulevard (Route 66). Its owners were William Tharp and his wife, Lecile; their daughter, famed dancer and choreographer Twyla Tharp, worked there while growing up. Moviegoers had to drive past the Tharps' car dealership to enter. Pacific Theatres operated the drive-in from 1972 until its 1988 shutdown. (Courtesy of American Classic Images.)

C.D. Weiser opened Yucca Valley's 1959 Sky Drive-in Theatre with 328 car spaces and in-car heaters. From 1961 until at least 1968, it employed one of the U.S.'s only female projectionists, Pauline Hanson. In 1971, the Sky began hosting a swap meet, which has continued long past the drive-in's 1994 closure. The Sky's ticket booth, marquee with neon stars, and some other features survive at 7028 Theatre Road. (Courtesy of the author.)

In the Mojave Desert's borax-mining company town of Trona, the multifunction, 1913 Austin Hall was the center of community life. In 1926, the American Potash and Chemical Corporation turned the arcaded, Mission Revival style building's central courtyard into a movie venue. Called the Trona Theatre, the unique airdrome featured bench seating for 800 people, floor-based steam heat, and a retractable, canvas cover for rainy periods. Harry Keller served as the open-air facility's projectionist for its entire lifespan. After the theatre gained sound equipment in 1931, Keller added midnight movies—playing them three nights a week until the venue's closure. (The photograph below shows workers at a midnight screening.) Along with films, the theatre hosted various community events. Movies ended there in 1954, when Trona's Fox Theatre opened. Austin Hall got demolished in 1965. (Both, courtesy of Searles Valley Historical Society.)

Trona's 636-seat Fox Theatre opened on November 18, 1954, playing *Desiree* in CinemaScope. Its grand opening marquee touted a "gala premiere" with "Hollywood stars in person" (which included Rita Moreno and Broderick Crawford). Fox West Coast designed it for Trona's desert environment in a fault zone—with an air filtration system, automatic-thermostat air conditioning, and supposedly earthquake-proof structural steel. Located on Main Street across from Austin Hall, the movie house featured a curved widescreen, surround-sound speakers, and swirling, floral murals and metalwork throughout. Later called Trona Theater and Trona Cinema, it shut down in 1991. A restaurant reused the lobby until around 2018; the back portion was storage space. As of spring 2022, the building sat boarded up. (Above, courtesy of American Classic Images; below, courtesy of Ken Kramer Collection, Margaret Herrick Library, Academy of Motion Picture Arts and Sciences.)

The Patio Theatre was an outdoor movie venue on Twentynine Palms' 1923 Smith's Ranch property. Bill and Prudie Underhill screened movies there and at the ranch's 1940 auditorium/gymnasium building—turning the projector around to serve both. The airdrome was still open in February 1956, when this flyer revealed it was playing second-run, 1955 movies. The Patio appears on a mural at 6298 Adobe Road. (Courtesy of Twentynine Palms Historical Society.)

Twentynine Palms' Clemons Drive-in Theatre—later renamed the Smith's Ranch Drive-in—opened in 1956. Designed by J. Arthur Drielsma for Art Clemons and DelDee Smith Clemons, it offered a playground, a 60-foot screen, 365 car spots, and 192 seats. Following a March 2020 to July 2022 closure due to the COVID-19 pandemic, the region's last operational, single-screen drive-in plays first-run movies on weekends. (Courtesy of Twentynine Palms Historical Society.)

The above photograph shows Bill and Prudie Underhill at the groundbreaking ceremony for their 29 Palms Theatre at 5712 Adobe Road. The $20,000 movie house opened on November 10, 1945, with *Johnny Angel*, starring George Raft. It featured 400 seats (including loges) and a sign with neon palm trees. Prudie frequently made the approximately 150-mile drive to Los Angeles to book films and get supplies, while daughter Ann (now Ann Congdon) grew up working in the snack bar. Over the years, the venue not only showed movies but held plays, meetings, beauty contests, etc. The Underhills closed the 29 Palms Theatre by March 1960. A furniture store later reused the freestanding, barrel-roof, reinforced concrete building. Today, a Marine-focused barbershop utilizes it. (Above, courtesy of Ann Congdon; below, courtesy of Twentynine Palms Historical Society.)

UNDERHILL'S   TWENTYNINE PALMS
STARLITE DRIVE-IN THEATRE

PHONE 367-4721 ANY HOUR FOR SHOW SCHEDULE

SCREEN 1   **SCREEN 2**

In March 1956, Bill and Prudie Underhill opened Twentynine Palms' Starlite Open Air Drive-in Theatre. It was located at 6215 Ocotillo Road, beside the Starlite Roller Rink—an outdoor facility that they had opened in 1952. The 400-car, 10-acre movie venue gained a second screen in 1958. Known as the Starlite Twin, it closed around 1988. An apartment complex stands on its site. (Courtesy of Ann Congdon.)

This postcard shows one of the book region's two operational, single-screen, indoor movie theaters. Originally named the Base Theater, it opened as part of Twentynine Palms' military base, the 1952 Marine Corps Training Center—now the Marine Corps Air Ground Combat Center. Along with regular movies, it has long offered plays, music, lectures, etc. Now called Sunset Cinema, it shows first-run films daily in 2D and 3D formats. (Courtesy of the author.)

Base Theater

Second Ave. looking North   Upland, Calif.   8

This postcard shows an oft-renamed movie house in Upland. Already operating by 1912 as the Lyric Theatre, it reopened as the Colonial following architect Homer W. Glidden's 1914 expansion and remodel (including Powers 6A projectors). Sold in 1930, the 418-seat venue became the Upland Theatre—a title it retained (except for a mid-1930s name change to the Studio) until its closure around 1951. The building is gone. (Courtesy of the author.)

The Grove Theatre's 1947 opening featured host Roddy McDowell. Western Amusement's Upland movie house offered 831 seats and a cry room. Its (mostly surviving) Streamline Moderne architecture included a 58-foot tower, over half a mile of neon, a circular ticket booth, and terrazzo. During the 1980s, it played Spanish-language films. A playhouse from 1991 until the COVID-19 pandemic's 2020 arrival, the Grove now hosts a church. (Courtesy of American Classic Images.)

"D" ST --- VICTORVILLE, CALIF. 2213

MESA THEATRE

THE FINEST THEATRE ON
THE DESERT

FIRST RUNS - - - SELECTED SHORTS

FURNACE HEATED

THREE COMPLETE SHOWS NIGHTLY
5:00, 7:00 and 9:00

•

Saturday Continuous From 2 P. M.

•

11c and 30c Until 6 P.M.

•

Sunday Continuous From 2 P. M.

TELEPHONE 2117   VICTORVILLE, CALIFORNIA

SECTION 562—P. L. & R. PERMIT NO. 12

CALIF.

The Victor Theatre's neon signage is visible in this postcard showing Victorville's D Street (Route 66). It showed films by 1917, when its projector got replaced. Blacks and Latinos sat in the balcony or back at the segregated, 320-seat venue. Western Amusement shuttered it in 1950 upon opening the El Rancho Theatre nearby. Its Halstead Building burned in 2010. (Courtesy of the California History Room, California State Library, Sacramento, California.)

The $25,000 Mesa Theatre's July 1936 opening advertisement touted it as "cool—comfortable—modern." Originally owned by John Roy, it was later part of Western Amusement. The 300-seat, air-conditioned, first-run movie house boasted Art Deco and Egyptian Revival architecture. During the Great Depression, it hosted talent contests, giveaways, and occasional Spanish-language films. Closing in May 1953, it no longer stands on 7th and C Streets. (Courtesy of California Route 66 Museum.)

SPECIAL PASS

ISSUED TO

MRS. ROSALIE WIESE

FOR USE AT THE

Joshua Drive-In Theatre

Frank E. Justice

Manager

VOID AFTER MAY 29, 1954

Opening in May 1953, the 400-car Joshua Drive-in Theatre was one of two Victorville drive-ins. The other was the twin-screen Balsam (1981–1987); Western Amusement's Jack Baldock operated both. Presumably named after the area's Joshua trees, the $75,000 Joshua was located on Seventh Street (Route 66) at Sand Street. Closing in 1982, it fell in 1989. The California Route 66 Museum has a replica marquee. (Courtesy of California Route 66 Museum.)

CINEMA 1
THE SOLDIER
CINEMA 2
ONE DARK NIGHT

EL RANCHO

Jack Baldock opened Victorville's 970-seat El Rancho Theatre for Western Amusement in June 1950. In 1953, the Modernist movie house (designed by Howard George Elwell) began offering CinemaScope and 3D. It got twinned in 1976. After briefly switching to Spanish-language and dubbed films, it closed in May 1984. A church later reused the theatre, which has sat vacant at 16856 C Street since at least 2019. (Courtesy of American Classic Images.)

Earl L. Pierce's 325-seat, $40,000 Yucaipa Theatre opened in January 1947 (above), playing the second-run, 1945 film *Song of Old Wyoming* with Simplex projectors. It was part of his Pierce Building at the corner of California Street and Avenue A in Yucaipa. Managed by H.W. "Red" Miller, the movie house's early advertisements promoted it as offering "good family entertainment." Pierce closed it for months in 1953 for a major remodeling and renovation, reopening it with first-run films, a new sound system, etc. In addition to showing movies, the Yucaipa Theatre hosted numerous community events over the years—ranging from Miss Yucaipa pageants to talent shows, holiday parties, and local associations' meetings. Ending its time as a film venue around 1965, the theatre's now-unrecognizable space has held various commercial uses since. (Both, courtesy of Yucaipa Valley Historical Society.)

Four

CITY OF SAN BERNARDINO

Dr. J.A. Patterson's 1936 Studio Theatre stood on Baseline Road. Walter L. Culver, Jr. designed its Art Deco architecture. The neighborhood movie house offered bicycle racks, parking, a smoking room, and air conditioning; a 35-foot widescreen was later added for CinemaScope. The 795-seat venue's upper level held restrooms but no balcony. The discount, second-run theatre closed around 1988 and was torn down in 2006. (Courtesy of San Bernardino County Museum.)

San Bernardino's Opera House, leased and managed by Martha L. Kiplinger for decades, showed films by 1910. Opened in 1882 by Herman Brinkmeyer and Kiplinger's father, James Waters, the red brick venue featured boxes, an orchestra, and approximately 900 seats. One of the city's main first-run movie theatres, it was demolished in 1927 for Court Street's expansion. (Courtesy of Security Pacific National Bank Photo Collection, Los Angeles Public Library.)

The Isis Theatre's sign is visible in the center-left, near City Hall, in this view of Third Street. The movie house opened in 1911 as the Family Theatre (which moved from another location). Renamed the Liberty in 1912, it soon became the Isis. The small, downscale Isis closed around 1932; its block was later razed. (Courtesy of Seaver Center for Western History Research, Los Angeles County Museum of Natural History.)

In 1904, the Broadway Theatre opened, showcasing vaudeville and motion pictures. It featured an orchestra, reserved seats, and box seats. Rechristened the Unique Theatre (above) in 1907, it got renamed the Savoy in 1913. The venue was remodeled in 1921 and renamed the Rialto (below), promoted as "San Bernardino's big family theatre." A 1930 fire caused another renovation. In 1947, the 700-seat movie house became "adults only," screening racy, much older films. It became the State Theatre in 1949. Despite being advertised as "good for the whole family," the State soon started hosting burlesque shows. Closing in 1951, its Third Street building was utilized by a church before its 1958 razing. (Both, courtesy of San Bernardino County Museum.)

The 1,200-seat West Coast Theatre opened on May 20, 1925, with vaudeville and the film *I Want My Man*. It was part of the new, $500,000 Platt Building at Fifth and E Streets. (Future U.S. president Lyndon B. Johnson worked as the office building's elevator operator at age 16, when the Texan briefly relocated to San Bernardino in 1925.) Designed by architects L.A. Smith and Howard E. Jones, the movie venue was originally run by its namesake, the West Coast Theatres circuit (later Fox West Coast). A major 1960 remodeling brought a CinemaScope screen and a new name: the Crest Theatre. Its reopening advertisement touted a "major studio feature preview," a "giant parade with Hollywood stars," and autographs. The venue multiplexed in 1972, its balcony hosting a second screen. The twin cinema's opening advertisement promoted an unnamed "major motion picture studio premiere" starring Bill Cosby and Robert Culp (presumably *Hickey and Boggs*). The Crest closed in 1989; the Platt Building fell in 1993, replaced by a parking lot. (Courtesy of American Classic Images.)

Advertised as "the Orange Empire's finest temple of amusement," the 1,855-seat Fox Theatre's September 1929 opening was unfortunately timed—the month before a stock market crash launched the Great Depression. Despite the Fox studio system's power and adding a free miniature golf course in the courtyard for moviegoers, the picture palace shut down in 1933. Its 1938 reopening boasted a sneak preview, *My Lucky Star*. Sometimes called the Fox Court (for its location at Court and D Streets), it closed by 1955, becoming the *San Bernardino Sun*'s storage warehouse. Since 2006, it has been reused as a banquet/event venue. Architects Balch and Stanbery's Mission Revival building still has some original elements. (Right, courtesy of California History Room, California State Library, Sacramento, California; below, courtesy of San Bernardino County Museum.)

On Mount Vernon Avenue (Route 66) at 7th Street, Sam Farah's Columbus Theatre opened in 1923. By 1930, the 600-seat Columbus had become a Spanish-language movie house; with a dance hall upstairs, it was a cultural nexus for the Mexican American community. Remodeled and renamed Teatro Azteca by 1938, it played Spanish-language films until at least 1983. It has sat vacant for decades. (Courtesy of American Classic Images.)

San Bernardino's independent Temple Theatre opened in 1909 on Third Street near F Street, receiving remodels in 1917 and 1939. Fox West Coast took over in 1941, shuttering the Temple around 1955. Reopening in 1959 as the 575-seat Capri Theatre, Fox's unprofitable arthouse venture closed in 1960. Its block and surrounding others got replaced by the 1972 Central City Mall, later Carousel Mall (demolished in 2023). (Courtesy of the author.)

Fox West Coast Theatres opened the 1,750-seat California Theatre in 1928 along Route 66 (at 562 West 4th Street). Architect John Paxton Perrine designed the picture palace, which still boasts Mission Revival and Spanish Colonial Revival architecture—plus its original Mighty Wurlitzer organ. In its early years, it hosted studio test screenings (including for *The Wizard of Oz* and *King Kong*); premieres; and famous performers. Since 1969, it has served as the California Theatre of the Performing Arts. (Above, courtesy of the California History Room, California State Library, Sacramento, California; below, courtesy of Ken Kramer Collection, Margaret Herrick Library, Academy of Motion Picture Arts and Sciences.)

Starting in 1910, E.H. Dowell's Auditorium Theatre played movies for 10¢ at 423 North E Street. (Dowell previously operated two other San Bernardino nickelodeons, the La Petite and the Star.) Carl Ray spent $10,000 to rehab, expand, and rename the 840-seat venue as the Strand in 1917. The Warner Bros. movie studio's theatre circuit added a Vitaphone sound system in 1930, reopening it as the Ritz. A 1941 remodel brought Art Deco architecture (seen here) and stadium seating. The Pussycat chain showed X-rated films there from approximately 1972 to 1991. (Owner Vincent Miranda was briefly jailed for public nuisance there in 1977.) The theatre's site has held a multiplex since 1999. (Courtesy of Theatre Historical Society of America, THS Theatre File Collection.)

In 1948, the 700-car Mount Vernon Motor-In Theatre opened—including a stage and windowed snack bar (for watching films while dining). A playground and swimming pool arrived in the 1950s. Demolished in 1972, the venue reopened in 1973 as the Mount Vernon Twin Drive-in. Closing in 1989, its lot holds a swap meet. (© Elisa Leonelli. Courtesy of Elisa Leonelli Collection, H.Mss.1102. Special Collections, The Claremont Colleges Library, Claremont, California.)

Statewide Theatres' freestanding, modernist Inland Cinema opened in 1967. Architects Tucker, Sadler, and Bennett designed its curved, glassy, fin-covered façade (still intact today). Ben Mayer Design Studios created its interior, including this postcard's mural. In 1974, its 1,232-seat auditorium, meant for screening 70mm films, was split into two. Inland Cinema closed around 1992; the building has since held commercial tenants. (Courtesy of Theatre Historical Society of America, Postcard Collection, PC-1970-062.)

Five

SAN GABRIEL VALLEY

South El Monte's Starlite Drive-in Theatre opened in 1950. Pacific Theatres soon took over the 860-car venue designed by J. Arthur Drielsma. The drive-in's swap meet continued past films' 1990s end until the COVID-19 pandemic's 2020 start. The 2540 Rosemead Boulevard property was purchased in 2023 for housing. The Googie-style marquee will remain. (© Elisa Leonelli. Courtesy of Elisa Leonelli Collection, H.Mss.1102. Special Collections, The Claremont Colleges Library, Claremont, California.)

The first of Alhambra's three venues named the Alhambra Theatre opened in 1912 at 101 East Main Street. Its Superba Theatre renaming occurred by May 1915. Per this 1921 program, the Superba exclusively showed Paramount films. The United Theatres of California circuit operated the movie house from 1922 until at least 1928 as the 450-seat United Theatre. A still-standing Art Deco building replaced it in 1934. (Courtesy of Homestead Museum Collection.)

The city's second Alhambra Theatre opened in 1917 on West Main Street. Renamed the Plaza in 1924, the 540-seat, white glazed-brick movie house quickly became the Granada (seen here circa 1928). Edwards Theatres dubbed it the Coronet in 1947, remodeling and changing it in 1963 into the Capri. Damage from the 6.6 magnitude, 1971 Sylmar Earthquake caused its razing. (Courtesy of Security Pacific National Bank Photo Collection, Los Angeles Public Library.)

O.W. Lewis left Alhambra's second Alhambra Theatre, opening the city's third movie house with that title around 1923. James Edwards bought the 952-seat venue (his second exhibition venture) around 1930. In 1940, he pioneered a type of multiplex, turning an adjacent building into a 325-seat auditorium. Despite sharing a box office, lobby, etc., the newer space got advertised separately—called the Annex or the Single Bill Theatre. Generally, both played the same double features at different times. The Annex closed in the 1950s, reopening around 1968 as the Gold Cinema. Edwards Theatres renamed the two, collectively, the Alhambra Twin Cinemas in the 1970s. The groundbreaking Main Street theatre got destroyed following 1987 earthquake damage. (Right, courtesy of Security Pacific National Bank Photo Collection, Los Angeles Public Library; below, courtesy of American Classic Images.)

Walter P. Temple opened Alhambra's $50,000 Temple Theatre on December 23, 1921. Walker and Eisen created its Mission Revival and Spanish Colonial revival architecture, offering 1,000 seats and a Wurlitzer organ. It became the El Rey Theatre around 1932. The 1950s brought a CinemaScope screen. Edwards Theatres gave the El Rey a major remodel (seen below) in the 1960s. After the 5.9 magnitude, 1987 Whittier Narrows earthquake caused the 333 West Main Street building major damage, it got demolished. (Above, courtesy of Harold A. Parker Studio Collection of Negatives, the Huntington Library, San Marino, California, photCL 402 [31208]; below, courtesy of American Classic Images.)

L.A. Smith designed Lou Bard's 1,100-seat, Egyptian Revival style, 1924 Bard's Garfield Egyptian Theatre. Later called the Garfield Theatre, it included a vaudeville stage and two cry rooms. 1929 brought it Vitaphone sound. From 1980 to 1995, Asian-language films played there, with its concession stand serving Chinese snacks. The façade of its ornate, $250,000 Valley Grand Building survives on Alhambra's Valley Boulevard at Garfield Avenue. (Courtesy of American Classic Images.)

The $20,000 Liberty Theatre opened in 1924 on Arcadia's Huntington Drive (Route 66). It had 500 seats, a pipe organ, and Simplex projectors in the projection room (which caught fire twice in 1925). Variously called the Liberty and the Arcadia Theatre, the latter name soon solidified. Edwards Theatres operated the Art Deco movie house when a 1942 fire ended its life. (Courtesy of Works Progress Administration Collection, Los Angeles Public Library.)

This 1977 photograph shows the demolition of Arcadia's Cinemaland Theatre, closed since 1975. It began as Edwards Theatres' $100,000 Santa Anita Theatre—providing 743 seats, a cry room, and 450 parking spaces. Its May 1942 opening included a parade and Hollywood celebrities. Remodeled and renamed in 1967, Cinemaland sat on Route 66 at Colorado Place and Huntington Drive, across from Santa Anita Park. (Courtesy of Arcadia Public Library, Arcadia, California.)

James Edwards's 1949 Edwards Drive-in Theatre, designed by S. Charles Lee, offered 400 car spaces (later expanded to 750). In 1967, Community Drive-in Church began holding Sunday services there. The $350,000 drive-in operated until at least 1992. Its 4445 Live Oak Avenue site in Arcadia hosts housing. (© Elisa Leonelli. Courtesy of Elisa Leonelli Collection, H.Mss.1102. Special Collections, The Claremont Colleges Library, Claremont, California.)

Principal Theatres' 625-seat, $35,000 Azusa Theatre opened with a 1927 world premiere, Will Rogers's *The Texas Steer*. Renamed the State Theatre in 1931, it advertised a celebrity-laden sneak preview in 1948. By 1953, it showed 3D films and Spanish-language movies often; the latter continued until at least 1962. Edwards Theatres retitled it the Village Theatre in 1963, razing it in 1972. (Courtesy of *Herald Examiner* Collection, Los Angeles Public Library.)

Azusa's 1,600-car, 1961 Azusa Foothill Drive-in Theatre sat on Foothill Boulevard (Route 66). When Azusa Pacific University bought it in 2001 for campus expansion, Los Angeles County had one other operational drive-in; Route 66 had no others west of Oklahoma. The Los Angeles Conservancy's preservation campaign and successful California Register of Historical Resources nomination saved the marquee. (Courtesy of Howard D. Kelly, Kelly-Holiday Mid-Century Aerial Collection, Los Angeles Public Library.)

The Edgewood Drive-in Theatre's June 15, 1955 "gala opening" advertisement promised "stars in person" and "first-run hits." The next year, its city—Baldwin Park—incorporated, while owner Aladdin Super Drive-in Theatres joined Pacific Theatres. A 1976 gang-related shooting at the 1,200-car Edgewood killed one person and injured two. Closing in 1985, its property is now a hospital. (Courtesy of Howard D. Kelly, Kelly-Holiday Mid-Century Aerial Collection, Los Angeles Public Library.)

The 1,700-car Vineland Drive-in Theatre opened in 1955 in the City of Industry (sometimes listed as Puente). Three more screens arrived in 1981. Following Pacific Theatres' COVID-19 pandemic-related bankruptcy, the Vineland stopped playing movies in 2022. (Its swap meet continued.) After a summer 2023 film series, with movies on Saturdays on one screen, its future is unclear. (Courtesy of Howard D. Kelly, Kelly-Holiday Mid-Century Aerial Collection, Los Angeles Public Library.)

Claremont's 500-seat, $30,000 Village Theatre, designed by Sumner Spaulding, opened in 1940. It was known for its weekly "college night;" its ticket booklets for children's movies on summer Saturdays; and, during the 1950s and beyond, being one of only a few arthouse theatres in either the San Gabriel Valley or Inland Empire. Closing in 1979, the movie house was converted into restaurants and stores. (Courtesy of Pitzer College Archives.)

W.C. Merwin's Isis Theatre opened on Covina's Badillo Avenue in 1910, advertising itself as "a high class motion picture parlor" catering "especially to women and children." It moved in 1911 beside the soon failed, 1911 Empress Theatre. In 1915, Lulu Dietz remodeled, renaming the Isis the Star Theatre. George Leonardy's movie house shuttered in 1921. The Star and Empress buildings stand at 217-219 North Citrus Avenue. (Courtesy of Covina Public Library.)

The Covina Theatre opened in 1921 in a former store in Covina. Frank Cox, architect of theatres in multiple states, designed the movie house for his relatives George Leonardy and Earl Sinks. Remodeled multiple times, the 499-seat venue closed in 1992, quickly becoming the Covina Valley Playhouse. The building, declared unsafe, was demolished in 2005. Its replacement, the Covina Center for the Performing Arts, has a replica marquee. (Courtesy of the author.)

The freestanding, 814-seat Fox Covina Theatre opened on June 24, 1969, with Disney's *The Love Bug*. Designed by Pearson & Wuesthoff for National General (Fox West Coast's successor), it became the 1,316-seat Fox Twin in 1972. Mann Theatres added a third screen in 1976. Later, it played second-run films and Indian, Hindi-language movies. Closing around 1999, the 211 North Azusa Avenue triplex is gone. (Courtesy of American Classic Images.)

C.E. Langford's 1959 Covina Drive-in Theatre, offering a playground and 400 car spaces, sat at Arrow Highway and Grand Avenue. Gaining a second screen in 1965, it became the Covina Twin. A church held services there in 1965–1967. Still showing movies in 1983, the theatre's land got rezoned for apartments in 1984. (Courtesy of UCSB Library Geospatial Collection, Flight C_23870, Frame 1253, May 12, 1960.)

Lou Berman's 1949 Big Sky Drive-in Theatre sat along Huntington Drive (Route 66) in what is now Duarte. Designed by J. Arthur Drielsma, the 650-car drive-in joined Pacific Theatres in 1953. The Big Sky operated until fall 1984, when the city's redevelopment agency bought it to build the Mountain Vista Plaza Shopping Center. (© Elisa Leonelli. Courtesy of Elisa Leonelli Collection, H.Mss.1102. Special Collections, The Claremont Colleges Library, Claremont, California.)

Arthur Sanborn opened the $110,000 El Monte Theatre in 1939. Featuring a free parking lot, air conditioning, 900 seats, and landscape murals, its Art Deco and Late Moderne design was by architect Earl T. Heitschmidt. Operated by Metropolitan Theatres after the Sanborn Theatres circuit left, the movie house showed Spanish-language films by 1984 (above). It became a twin-screen facility later in the 1980s. During the 1990s, it offered Spanish-subtitled movies, later switching to Latino-oriented plays and performances. Boarded up by 2003, its building on Main Street (originally Valley Boulevard, then Valley Mall) got converted to commercial usage. The theatre's "El Monte" blade sign survives. (Above, courtesy of American Classic Images; below, courtesy of Tom B'hend and Preston Kaufmann Collection, Margaret Herrick Library, Academy of Motion Picture Arts and Sciences.)

S. Charles Lee designed the 1939 Tumbleweed Theatre, one of Southern California's most architecturally distinctive movie houses. Located on Garvey Avenue in El Monte's rural Five Points neighborhood, Edwards Theatres' $35,000 Tumbleweed matched its setting; a *Motion Picture Herald* article called it a "farm theater for farm-minded folk." The tower sign resembled a windmill, complete with a revolving topper. A wagon wheel-adorned fence held a supposed farmyard with a pond and a wishing well. The auditorium featured wooden beams, wagon wheel-shaped chandeliers, and Western murals. The rustic, 750-seat venue provided a cry room. Operating until at least 1961, the Tumbleweed was razed by 1970. (Both, courtesy of S. Charles Lee Papers, UCLA Library Special Collections, Charles E. Young Research Library, University of California, Los Angeles.)

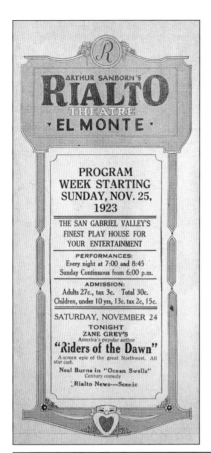

Walker and Eisen designed El Monte's 700-seat, $50,000 Rialto Theatre. Arthur Sanborn managed (then owned) owner Walter P. Temple's 1923 venue. In 1940, James Edwards bought it. Renamed the Valley Theatre by 1942, it played Spanish-language movies twice weekly in 1951. Edwards Theatres closed it by 1954. The Main Street building survives. (Courtesy of Tom B'hend and Preston Kaufmann Collection, Margaret Herrick Library, Academy of Motion Picture Arts and Sciences.)

Costing $300,000, the 1948 El Monte Drive-in Theatre boasted an elaborate mural on one of America's largest screens (70 feet tall). In a 1949 national theatre signage contest, its Streamline Moderne marquee won first prize for creator B.F. Shearer. Pacific Theatres' 900-car drive-in played Spanish-language movies from 1982 until at least 1988. Later showing Hollywood productions again, it closed around 1998 and fell. (Courtesy of Library of Congress, LC-MA05-299 [P&P].)

Glendora's 600-seat, $50,000 Mission Theatre, designed by J. Cyrill Bennett, opened in 1923 at 108 West Foothill Boulevard (Route 66). In 1931, new owners Richard and Maurice McDonald renamed it the Beacon Theatre. The brothers sold it in 1938 (opening their first McDonald's restaurant in 1940 in San Bernardino). Later called the Glendora Theatre, films ended in 1967 before its 1968 teardown for supermarket construction. (Courtesy of Glendora Historical Society.)

Projection engineers George Reid and William Spencer opened Glendora's 374-seat Plaza Theatre in a converted post office in 1971. It utilized their technology, which let an employee run a push-button projector from the concession stand/box office. The movie house's mostly residential setting at 175 North Vermont Avenue proved a drawback; some advertisements even included a map. Closed by 1983, its building holds commercial uses. (Courtesy of American Classic Images.)

The 599-seat Puente Theatre opened in 1947 in La Puente (originally unincorporated Puente). S. Charles Lee's design included a Lamella roof and a star-topped tower. In 1948, owners Steve and Emma Chorak sued multiple film distributors and local circuits, making monopoly and antitrust accusations; they lost. Renamed the Star Theatre by 1957, the venue showed Spanish-language fare in the 1970s. X-rated films screened there from 1978 to 2000, when it lost its permit amid lewd conduct and prostitution claims. Renovated in 2001, it hosted first-run movies (some with Spanish subtitles), plus Latino-oriented events like Lucha Libre matches. Closing in 2007, a developer demolished it in 2019 despite preservation efforts. The Los Angeles Historic Theatre Foundation saved its neon star. (Both, courtesy of S. Charles Lee Papers, UCLA Library Special Collections, Charles E. Young Research Library, University of California, Los Angeles.)

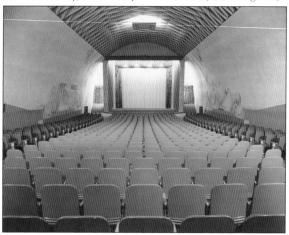

On Route 66 (Foothill Boulevard) near White Avenue in La Verne, the Mount Baldy Drive-in's animated neon marquee depicted the theatre's namesake ski resort. The 1200-car drive-in opened on June 9, 1960, with a 100-foot-tall, 70-foot-wide screen. It closed in 1984, replaced by a post office. The nearby Los Angeles County Fair reused and then saved the marquee, which is in storage. (Courtesy of Library of Congress, LC-MA05- 6088 [P&P].)

This photograph shows the Monrovia Days parade passing Myrtle Avenue's Elite Theatre. The 400-seat Monrovia Opera House operated from approximately 1897 to 1908, then became the Elite. In September 1910, W.O. Wheelan remodeled, reopening it as the Imp Theatre—advertising "high class motion pictures, illustrated songs, and vaudeville." New manager W.K. Wyman brought the Elite moniker back in December; Elite advertisements still appeared in 1913. (Courtesy of Monrovia Historical Society.)

In 1920, Monrovia's existing Colonial Theatre moved to a new building at 316 South Myrtle Avenue. After temporarily closing due to the Great Depression, the movie house got renamed the Monrovia Theatre by 1937. In 1941, Fox West Coast bought the 500-seat Monrovia, which operated until at least 1948. The building, greatly altered, has held retail since 1957. (Courtesy of Frashers Fotos Collection/HJG and Pomona Public Library, Pomona, California.)

The $200,000 Lyric Theatre's 1925 opening featured Rin Tin Tin's appearance, vaudeville, and film (with Wurlitzer organ accompaniment). Wilson, Merrill, and Wilson designed the segregated, 1,210-seat picture palace's Spanish Colonial Revival architecture. Renamed the Crest in 1962, it became the Crest Twin in 1973, then played X-rated movies in 1974. Monrovia condemned it in 1978. (Courtesy of Southern California Edison Photographs and Negatives, the Huntington Library, San Marino, California, 02-21506.)

Montebello's Star Theatre marquee promoted the 1926 film *Let's Get Married* in this photograph. The 1915, arched-entry building hosted the Star by 1924—when its manager placed an advertisement in Montebello High School's time capsule. The 240-seat Star closed in 1931, reopened with 280 seats, then shut again by 1933. It still stands at 520 West Whittier Boulevard. (Courtesy of Security Pacific National Bank Photo Collection, Los Angeles Public Library.)

In this 1946 photograph, Montebello's Frontier Days parade passed the Vogue Theatre at 712 West Whittier Boulevard. A 1929 Hudson car dealership became the Vogue in 1937 (using items owner Al Olander took from his 1935 Cameo Theatre nearby). S. Charles Lee gave the 500-seat, second-run showplace Streamline Moderne elements. Closing around 1966, the Vogue's building has long held commercial uses. (Courtesy of Lucille Stewart Collection, Los Angeles Public Library.)

Like at his older Vogue Theatre, co-owner Al Olander had architect S. Charles Lee design Montebello's 1950 Garmar Theatre (named after Olander's sons, Gary and Mark). The freestanding Garmar was meant to catch motorists' eyes, featuring vibrant Modernist architecture—with a massive marquee; neon name signage atop the Lamella barrel roof; and a façade covered in 30 neon-lit, steel circles. The $250,000 movie house also featured 1,000 seats, a 400-car parking lot, a Cycloramic screen, a vaudeville stage, pull-lever vending machines at the concession stand, a cry room, and a smoking room (below). Operating until 1981, the 2325 W. Whittier Blvd building was torn down in 1983 for the Garmar Plaza strip mall. (Both, courtesy of S. Charles Lee Papers, UCLA Library Special Collections, Charles E. Young Research Library, University of California, Los Angeles.)

C.A. Howe and G.G. Merrill opened Monterey Park's Mission Theatre in March 1925. By May, West Coast Theatres took over the venue, which offered 875 seats, a Wurlitzer organ, and Mission Revival architecture by Leonard L. Jones. Future mogul James Edwards began his career there, buying it in 1930 as his first movie house. Reopening it with sound as the Monterey Theatre, he and his wife, Bernice, ran it. A CinemaScope screen arrived after Ed Wood shot *Jail Bait* scenes there in 1954. Edwards Theatres shut the second-run venue in 1979 (upon opening the Monterey Mall Cinema triplex nearby). A lessee played Asian-language films until the 1987 Whittier Narrows earthquake caused damage. The city condemned the theatre, denying its owners' renovation plans. (Above, courtesy of Security Pacific National Bank Photo Collection, Los Angeles Public Library; right, courtesy of American Classic Images.)

Monterey Park's Floral Drive-in Theatre (often listed as being in East Los Angeles) opened in August 1950 with a "major studio preview" and "stars in person." In 1962, the theatre advertised that it played Spanish-language films three days a week. Its screenings soon switched completely, as this program flyer for the "Floral Autocine" shows. Pacific Theatres operated the Floral for decades, until at least 1981. It later disappeared. (Courtesy of the author.)

Pomona's Belvedere Theatre opened at 255 South Garey Avenue in September 1911, advertising "a good show" with "moving pictures" and vaudeville. In the early 1920s, the Belvedere appeared in the *Year Book* trade journal's annual lists of the nation's "Important First Run Houses." After remodeling, its 1926 grand reopening presented a world premiere, *Young April*. A 1933 fire ended the 800-seat Belvedere's life. (Courtesy of Pomona Public Library, Pomona, California.)

Fox West Coast's 1941 State Theatre sat on the Belvedere Theatre's former lot. Its opening feature, *Golden Hoofs*, was partially shot at Pomona's Los Angeles County Fairgrounds. Clifford A. Balch designed the 502-seat, $33,000 movie house's Art Deco architecture. From around 1957 to early 1962, it played Spanish-language double features every Tuesday. The 1963 Home Savings and Loan's parking lot replaced it. (Courtesy of Legacy Photo Collection, Los Angeles Public Library.)

Howard Hughes's Hughes-Franklin circuit opened Pomona's $50,000 Sunkist Theatre in 1931. Named after the local citrus cooperative's brand, the Sunkist's Spanish Colonial Revival design was by S. Charles Lee. It offered 874 seats, valet parking, and an automatic drinking fountain. Fox West Coast took over in 1932. The Sunkist showed Spanish-language films weekly by 1953. Shuttering in 1955, its Garey Avenue building became offices. (Courtesy of Pomona Public Library, Pomona, California.)

The Fox Theatre opened in 1931 with the world premiere of *Six Cylinder Love*, starring special guest Spencer Tracy. Fox West Coast created the 1,751-seat, $300,000, Art Deco picture palace as a test-screening site. Designed by Balch and Stanbery, the Fox's tower had "Preview" signage; locals evaluated pre-release films inside an "atmospheric" auditorium under silver-lined clouds. After the Fox closed in 1976, the city leased it for performing arts—which failed quickly. From 1980 to 1993, the Fox played Spanish-language films. After a church stint, a new lessee brought rap shows and raves in 1998. Interior damage, two murders, a downtown riot, and a city-mandated shutdown resulted. Pomona purchased the landmarked Fox in 2002, selling it to preservation-oriented developers in 2007. Following a $10 million restoration, it reopened in 2009 as a concert venue. (Both, courtesy of Pomona Public Library, Pomona, California.)

Pomona's 1923 California Theatre opened with Buster Keaton attending *Hospitality*'s world premiere. West Coast Theatres' 1,275-seat, Egyptian Revival picture palace sat vacant 1932-1936. Retitled the United Artists Theatre in 1949, a sneak preview reopened it. Playing Spanish-language movies in the 1970s, it then became the Pomona Valley Auditorium. A church reuses its 235 West 3rd Street building. (Courtesy of Frashers Fotos Collection / HJG and Pomona Public Library, Pomona, California.)

This 1971 Flack Theatres pass was valid at Rowland Heights' 5th Avenue Theatre, which Jack and Eleanor Flack opened in June 1969 in a still-extant strip mall on 5th Avenue (now 18363 Colima Road). From December 1973 to at least August 1974, new operator George Voss's renamed Rowland Heights Theatre played X-rated films. Raids, reel seizures, and a court case led to the adult venue's closure. (Courtesy of the author.)

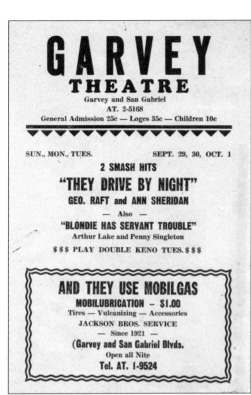

GARVEY

THEATRE

Garvey and San Gabriel
AT. 2-5168
General Admission 25c — Loges 35c — Children 10c

▼▼▼▼▼▼▼▼▼▼▼▼▼▼

SUN., MON., TUES.   SEPT. 29, 30, OCT. 1

2 SMASH HITS

"THEY DRIVE BY NIGHT"
GEO. RAFT and ANN SHERIDAN

— Also —

"BLONDIE HAS SERVANT TROUBLE"
Arthur Lake and Penny Singleton

$ $ $ PLAY DOUBLE KENO TUES. $ $ $

AND THEY USE MOBILGAS
MOBILUBRICATION — $1.00
Tires — Vulcanizing — Accessories
JACKSON BROS. SERVICE
— Since 1921 —
(Garvey and San Gabriel Blvds.
Open all Nite
Tel. AT. 1-9524

Edwards Theatres opened the 1937 Garvey Theatre on Garvey Avenue in the unincorporated Garvey area (now part of Rosemead). It offered 750 seats, a parking lot, and a cry room. The second-run movie house closed around 1952. It then hosted a church; showed films again by 1963; had another church reuse; and got razed. (Courtesy of Tom B'hend and Preston Kaufmann Collection, Margaret Herrick Library, Academy of Motion Picture Arts and Sciences.)

The 1938 Rosemead Theatre opened in a former store on Rosemead's Valley Boulevard. S. Charles Lee planned the $50,000 conversion for Edwards Theatres. The 800-seat movie house had a free parking lot. Remodeled in 1947, it was still operating in 1952. Retail usage (a market) soon returned to the later-destroyed building. (Courtesy of S. Charles Lee Papers, UCLA Library Special Collections, Charles E. Young Research Library, University of California, Los Angeles.)

The Robert L. Lippert circuit's 700-seat Canyon Theatre opened in 1966 in San Dimas's Canyon Center. Gene Harvey and his wife, Judy (seen here), owned it from 1973 onward. In the 1990s, the Canyon was known for regularly screening the *Rocky Horror Picture Show*, foreign films, and classic movies. After playing *Titanic* for 13 weeks, the Harveys' movie house closed in 1998. Its strip mall later fell. (Courtesy of San Dimas Historical Society.)

San Gabriel's 1927 Mission Playhouse boasts Mission Revival and Spanish Colonial Revival architecture. The Great Depression ended performances there; the 1,490-seat theatre hosted only movies from 1932 to 1945. Since then, it has been a performing arts venue. Called the San Gabriel Civic Auditorium until 2007, then retitled the Mission Playhouse again, it screens silent movies weekly. (Courtesy of Frashers Fotos Collection/HJG and Pomona Public Library, Pomona, California.)

When Edwards Theatres opened the San Gabriel Theatre at 330 West Las Tunas Drive in San Gabriel in 1942, it was the city's second movie venue by that name. The first San Gabriel Theatre began with owner John Feldmiller regularly projecting films inside a tent in 1911. It then moved into a purpose-built, 200-seat, Mission Revival style building onsite (at Mission Road and Angeleno Avenue) in 1912. That San Gabriel Theatre closed around 1932, when the Mission Playhouse started showing movies. The new, 600-seat, mostly second-run San Gabriel Theatre was designed by Clifford A. Balch. Renaming it the Century Theatre in 1967, Edwards shut it down in 1979. The movie house soon reopened as the Kuo Hwa Theater, with a lessee playing Asian-language films there until 1993. The operator then moved, opening the twin-screen Kuo Hwa Cinemas as part of a new, Chinese-oriented shopping center nearby; that 625-seat multiplex survived from 1994 to 1998. Meanwhile, the original Kuo Hwa quickly became the Bridge Theater, which continued playing Asian movies until 1995. The building then got razed. (Courtesy of American Classic Images.)

The San Gabriel Drive-in Theatre, a partnership between Edwards Theatres and Cal Pac (Pacific Theatres), opened in 1955 on Valley Boulevard. J. Arthur Drielsma's design had 1,100 car spaces, a playground, a Google-style marquee, and business offices for Edwards. In 1967–1968, a drive-in church operated there weekly. The theatre's movie listings disappeared after December 1986. It later fell. (Courtesy of Security Pacific National Bank Photo Collection, Los Angeles Public Library.)

Sierra Madre's 230-seat Wisteria Theatre (sometimes called the Wistaria) opened inside a 1910 store building in 1924, screening *The Virginian*. The Great Depression caused its 1931–1940 vacancy. Renamed the Sierra Madre Theatre in 1943, it was the arthouse Bogart Theatre in 1968–1971. The Sierra Madre Playhouse has operated there since 1979. The venue has appeared in TV and film, including the 2023 blockbuster *Oppenheimer*. (Courtesy of Sierra Madre Historical Archives.)

West Coast Theatres' 1925 Rialto Theatre opened along Route 66 (Fair Oaks Avenue) with a world premiere, *What Happened to Jones?*, attended by the movie's star and director. Designed by L.A. Smith, South Pasadena's Moorish style picture palace featured 1,200 seats, a Wurlitzer organ-led orchestra, and vaudeville. Amid a 1970s campaign to prevent a redevelopment agency from replacing it with parking, it received local, state, and federal landmark designations; a preservation group, Friends of the Rialto, formed in 1983. After playing Spanish-language fare, the Rialto got a new operator, Landmark Theatres, in 1976. It showed arthouse films, classics, Oscar nominees, etc. until 2007. In 2017, a church moved into the ornate, intact showplace (which has appeared in numerous movies). The Friends nonprofit organization and the Rialto's owners finished an exterior restoration in 2021. (Both, courtesy of South Pasadena Public Library.)

South Pasadena's Ritz Theatre sat at 804 Fair Oaks Avenue (Route 66). The 700-seat Ritz was a 1936 renaming of the 1916 Colonial Theatre, which Edward J. Borgmeyer had designed for Edward Jarecki. In 1944, the Ritz held a war bond drive. Despite Edwards Theatres giving the movie house a 1956 refurbishing, including a CinemaScope screen, it closed the next year. The building is gone. (Courtesy of South Pasadena Public Library.)

S. Charles Lee designed Edwards Theatres' 1940 Temple Theatre with a mix of Cape Cod, Colonial Revival, and Art Deco architecture. *Boxoffice* called it "one of the most unique theatres in the United States." The 750-seat movie house operated on Temple City's Las Tunas Drive until 1982. (Town founder Walter P. Temple owned multiple movie theatres.) The four-screen Edwards Temple Cinema—now demolished—replaced it onsite. (Courtesy of American Classic Images.)

The $500,000 Eastland Theatre's November 1961 opening featured an "invitational premiere"—with Jayne Mansfield attending. (Invitees presumably watched Mansfield's *The George Raft Story*, released later that month.) Designed by Smith and Williams, Arthur Sanborn's Eastland was a Modernist, 70mm-equipped, 1,000-seat movie house in West Covina's Eastland Shopping Center parking lot. It added two screens in 1976, then two more in 1981. Going dark in 1999, the Eastland is gone. (Courtesy of the author.)

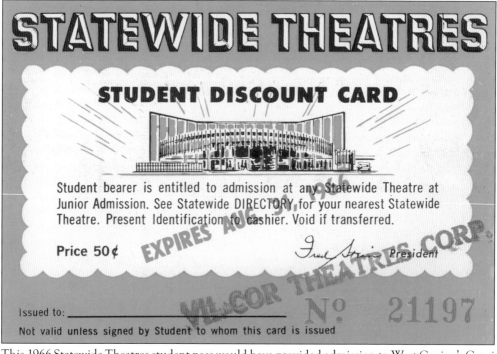

This 1966 Statewide Theatres student pass would have provided admission to West Covina's Capri Theatre, which the circuit opened in June 1963 with *Bye Bye Birdie*. The freestanding, Modernist venue offered 800 seats, a 300-car parking lot, and a widescreen for 70mm films. In 1980, the 444 South Glendora Avenue theatre was remodeled into a three-screen facility, the Capri Triplex. Closing later in the 1980s, it got demolished. (Courtesy of the author.)

Six

CITY OF PASADENA

Warner's Photoplay opened in August 1914 in a remodeled building at 28 East Colorado Boulevard (Route 66) in Pasadena. Owner Henry Warner was not related to Warner Bros. Pasadena High School's 1914–1915 yearbook promoted it as a "cool and comfortable" theatre offering afternoon movies aimed at students. Following a 1927 explosion and fire, another structure replaced the Photoplay in 1930. (Courtesy of the Archives at Pasadena Museum of History, T2-35.)

The first of three Crown Theatres in Pasadena opened in 1909. (The others are the former Raymond Theatre and a current dance studio/event venue.) A 1910 advertisement touted its "first-class pictures and vaudeville" for 10¢. The Crown was still operating in 1928 at 29 West Colorado Boulevard. In 1929, the site's present Art Deco building replaced it. (Courtesy of the Archives at Pasadena Museum of History, Flag_3-21-128.)

In 1911, multimillionaire W.H. Clune opened Clune's Pasadena Theatre with live entertainment. Clune's screened films by 1915, when an African American association protested *The Birth of a Nation* showing there. Clifford A. Balch gave the 1,194-seat theatre a Mission Revival remodel in 1930 for Fox West Coast. The renamed Fox Pasadena closed in 1953. Its 61 West Colorado Boulevard building holds stores. (Courtesy of Legacy Photo Collection, Los Angeles Public Library.)

Fisher's Theatre, a performance venue, was operating by 1910 at 85 North Fair Oaks Avenue. By 1913, it became a burlesque showplace, the Savoy—which turned into the Pasadena Community Playhouse around 1917. The acting troupe left the building for the current Pasadena Playhouse in 1925. Architect Walter C. Folland remodeled the facility for films; it soon reopened as the 444-seat Fair Oaks Theatre. A 1945 fire caused another remodel and a new name, the Oaks Theatre. In 1959, owner Harold E. Wenzler started showing X-rated movies there. He later added a 30-seat auditorium upstairs, the Tom Kat, playing gay porn. Despite multiple arrests of Wenzler and other staff, plus various lawsuits by Wenzler, the Oaks remained adults-only until its 1977 demolition for Parsons Engineering's headquarters. (Above, courtesy of Pasadena Playhouse Archives; right, courtesy of Pasadena Public Library, Pasadena, California.)

Frank Dale opened Pasadena's $26,000 Strand Theatre in 1914. Following a Spanish-style 1924 remodeling, the 900-seat venue was known for its marketing displays. It closed around 1956 as the Fox Strand. It and other buildings along West Colorado Boulevard's 300 block were replaced in 1980 by Plaza Pasadena, a now-demolished indoor mall. (Courtesy of Harold A. Parker Studio Collection of Negatives, the Huntington Library, San Marino, California, photCL 402 [31928].)

Part of an apartment/retail building at 845 East Washington Boulevard, the 900-seat Washington Theatre opened in 1925, premiering *Eve's Lover*. Renamed Cinema 21 in 1968, it became one of Southern California's only African American–owned theatres upon Ralph Riddle's 1972 purchase. It ran Black-oriented movies, then Spanish-language and adult films, until 1989. The auditorium sits unused in the landmarked, rehabbed structure. (Courtesy of the Archives at Pasadena Museum of History, T2-12.)

D.H. Schumann's $45,000 Florence Theatre, designed by O.P. Dennis, opened in 1918. In 1928, it started playing talkies. James Edwards remodeled the 797-seat movie house, renaming it the State, in 1935. A 1938 fire followed. The State joined the Pussycat Theatres circuit in 1984, showing adult films until 1989. Asian-language movies screened there briefly. Repertory, independent, and documentary films were popular there later. Owner Gene Harvey closed the State Theatre in 2000. The Museum of Neon Art took its sign. The Florence Theatre's original, terra cotta-accented façade is visible, uncovered during the 770 East Colorado Boulevard building's expansion. (Above, courtesy of Harold A. Parker Studio Collection of Negatives, the Huntington Library, San Marino, California, photCL 402 [31508]; below, courtesy of the Archives at Pasadena Museum of History, PSN State Theater 1986.)

Jensen's Raymond Theatre, a 2,200-seat, vaudeville/film venue, opened in 1921 at 129 North Raymond Avenue. Prominent Pasadena architect J. Cyril Bennett designed the $500,000, Beaux Arts structure for Henry Christian Jensen. In 1948, renamed the Crown Theatre, it received a $100,000 modernization. The Crown's X-rated *Deep Throat* screening caused protests and a city lawsuit in 1973–1974. The auditorium held concerts from 1980 to 1988; called Perkins Palace, it hosted everyone from Bruce Springsteen and Fleetwood Mac to Tina Turner. After developers bought the theatre, the Friends of the Raymond organization formed in 1987. Following a lengthy preservation campaign, a mixed-use development incorporated the partially restored building in 2008. (Left, courtesy of Harold A. Parker Studio Collection of Negatives, the Huntington Library, San Marino, California, photCL 402 [28571]; below, courtesy of the Archives at Pasadena Museum of History, T2-10d.)

In 1925, Henry Warner opened Warner's Egyptian Theatre in Pasadena's Lamanda Park neighborhood. Kenneth A. Gordon designed the $165,000 theatre's Egyptian Revival architecture (including a sunray-topped proscenium and scarab designs). The 800-seat venue initially featured a cry room, vaudeville, and first-run movies. By 1935, when Warner closed his theatre, it was playing fourth-run films for small audiences. Gus Metzger and his nephew, Universal Pictures' general manager Louis B. Metzger, leased it—replacing its seats, screen, equipment, marquee, etc. The movie house reopened as the Uptown Theatre in 1936. Its historic façade was covered by 1964. After the Uptown's 1980s closing, its lobby held retail. The 2316 East Colorado Boulevard theatre sits vacant, its auditorium mostly intact. (Above, courtesy of Harold A. Parker Studio Collection of Negatives, the Huntington Library, San Marino, California, photCL 402 [32092]; below, courtesy of American Classic Images.)

Pasadena's only historic theatre showing movies today is the six-screen Regency Academy Cinemas at 1003 East Colorado Boulevard. The now unrecognizable, Route 66 multiplex's life began in 1925 as the 1,709-seat Bard's Egyptian Theatre. Architect L.A. Smith created its Egyptian Revival design for Lou Bard. It later became Bard's Colorado, then the Fox Colorado. In 1942, Fox West Coast gave the picture palace a Streamline Moderne remodel, renaming it the Academy Theatre. Carl G. Moeller did a 1958 modernization, adding an elevator. The Academy frequently held test screenings (including for *The Music Man*); the films' stars often attended. It got multiplexed in 1986. The balcony gained two screens; the original auditorium was split into four. (Above, courtesy of Harold A. Parker Studio Collection of Negatives, the Huntington Library, San Marino, California, photCL 402 [31478]; below, courtesy of American Classic Images.)

Vacant in this 1955 photograph, the Park Theatre closed around 1951. The neighborhood movie house on North Fair Oaks Avenue opened on Christmas 1928. Designed by Dallas firm Orlopp and Orlopp for Texas-based circuit Robb and Rowley, the 760-seat Park offered parking and a "washed air cooling system." Per an oral history on Pasadena African American life, the venue was rare in allowing Black attendees in the 1920s and 1930s. (Courtesy of Bison Archives.)

As this photograph reveals, the 1930 Tower Theatre had a major disadvantage. Its building on Colorado Boulevard near Fair Oaks Avenue was adjacent to Santa Fe Railroad tracks; former patrons recalled passing trains causing earthquake-like shaking. Still, the 754-seat Tower operated into the early 1950s. The Art Deco structure by local architect B.G. Horton was demolished for a parking lot. (Courtesy of Herman J. Schultheis Collection, Los Angeles Public Library.)

This image shows the United Artists Theatre's concession stand. (The 1931 movie house's exterior is on the book cover.) Along with providing snacks, it also served as a marketing site, here promoting not only 1950 tropical musical *Pagan Love Song* but United flights to Hawaii. Architect Clifford A. Balch and the Walker and Eisen firm created the theatre's Art Deco design. (Courtesy of the Archives at Pasadena Museum of History, JAH6301.)

The 748-seat, arthouse Colorado Theatre launched in 1949 with *The Mozart Story*. Clarence J. Smale designed the $80,000, modernist, Quonset hut-style structure with a vaulted roof of Lamella wooden trusses. Operator Laemmle closed the arthouse venue in 2001 (two years after Laemmle's Playhouse 7 opened nearby). A church has since utilized the theatre building at 2588 East Colorado Boulevard. (Courtesy of Theatre Historical Society of America, THS Theatre File Collection.)

In 1964, arthouse chain Laemmle turned a pizza parlor at 2670 East Colorado Boulevard into the Esquire Theatre. Designed by movie art director Eugene Lourie, the 525-seat movie house was known for film festivals, classic film screenings, and performances. Laemmle shuttered it in 1999 after opening the Playhouse 7. The structure holds retail. (Courtesy of Tom B'hend and Preston Kaufmann Collection, Margaret Herrick Library, Academy of Motion Picture Arts and Sciences.)

In this photograph, a Rose Parade float passes the Venus Adult Theatre's second location. Opened by Donald Goulet at 2226 East Colorado Boulevard on July 25, 1969, the Venus added a second screen by 1976. After a 1980s move to 964 East Colorado, it closed around 1989. Despite raids, arrests, and controversy, the Venus was the longest lasting of Pasadena's multiple X-rated movie houses. (Courtesy of the Pasadena Public Library, Pasadena, California.)

The Hastings Drive-in Theatre opened on May 11, 1950, with appearances by celebrities Roy Rogers, Dale Evans, and their horse Trigger. Located at Foothill Boulevard and Rosemead Boulevard in the Hastings Ranch neighborhood, it held 1,000 cars. The drive-in featured a color-changing marquee, a playground, and a rideable train for children. It closed in September 1968. (Courtesy of the Archives at Pasadena Museum of History, J. Allen Hawkins Collection, 69020.)

In 1968, part of the Hastings Drive-in's parking lot was replaced by the Pasadena Hastings Theatre. The Sterling Recreation Organization's 1,500-seat venue, designed by Roland Decker Pierson, played Cinerama and 70mm films. Pacific Theatres' 1985 expansion turned it into a five-screen multiplex. It became the Hastings 8 in 1994. Closing in 2007, the movie house was demolished. (Courtesy of the Archives at Pasadena Museum of History, PSN Theatres–Pasadena Hastings Theater.)

INDEX

Discover Thousands of Local History Books
Featuring Millions of Vintage Images

Arcadia Publishing, the leading local history publisher in the United States, is committed to making history accessible and meaningful through publishing books that celebrate and preserve the heritage of America's people and places.

Find more books like this at
www.arcadiapublishing.com

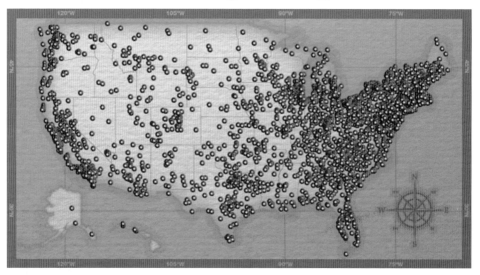

Search for your hometown history, your old stomping grounds, and even your favorite sports team.

Consistent with our mission to preserve history on a local level, this book was printed in South Carolina on American-made paper and manufactured entirely in the United States. Products carrying the accredited Forest Stewardship Council (FSC) label are printed on 100 percent FSC-certified paper.

MADE IN THE USA